HOUSE CALLS

HOUSE CALLS

The Memoirs of a Country Doctor

Marvin Brown, M.D.

Prometheus Books
Essex, Connecticut

Ⓟ Prometheus Books
An imprint of The Globe Pequot Publishing Group, Inc.
64 South Main Street
Essex, CT 06426
www.globepequot.com

Copyright © 1988 by Marvin Brown

All rights reserved. No part of this book may be reproduced in any form or by any electronic or mechanical means, including information storage and retrieval systems, without written permission from the publisher, except by a reviewer who may quote passages in a review.

Library of Congress Cataloging-in-Publication Data

Brown, Marvin, 1912–
    House calls.
    1. Brown, Marvin, 1912–   . 2. Physicians (General practice)—New York (State)—Biography. 3. Medicine, Rural—New York (State) I. Title.
R154.B8595A3   1988 610'.92'4 [B]   88-4076
ISBN 978-0-87975-448-8

Dedicated to the memory of my beloved wife, Bee, whose support, devotion, and inspiration have provided me with the courage and strength to fulfill my career as a Country Doctor—and whose love I cherished every day of our almost fifty years together.

May her memory and the memoirs found in the pages of this book be a source of inspiration to our beloved grandchildren—Courtney, Betsy, Amy, Eric, Nathaniel, Jennifer, Lauren, Deborah, Dana, and Carrie, and to our foster grandsons Peter, Eric, and George Frey.

Contents

Foreword		9
Chapter One	Arrival	13
Chapter Two	Settling In	23
Chapter Three	A Hard Day's Night	33
Chapter Four	Placebos and Mudholes	49
Chapter Five	A Little Help from My Colleagues	65
Chapter Six	Family Affairs	75
Chapter Seven	The War Years	93
Chapter Eight	Advances and Changes	103
Chapter Nine	A Sister and Daughter	127
Chapter Ten	Labors of Love	141
Chapter Eleven	Bee's Illness	159
Afterword		211
Bibliography		213

Foreword

For forty-three years and ten months, I practiced medicine as a general practitioner and family practitioner in a small village in upstate New York. I treated young and old, rich and poor, farmers, politicians, business men, laborers. I soothed baby rashes and treated sore throats, battled pneumonia and set broken limbs. I brought patients into the world and tried hard to ease their passage out of it. To do these things I traveled over an area of almost four hundred square miles by car, sleigh, and snowshoe. I was "on call" around the clock, spending countless nights tending patients in lonely farmhouses on dirt roads.

Over those years, my wife and I raised four sons and took to our hearts a special foster daughter. We made many friends and tried to become useful members of our community. We fought the good fight on the home front during World War II and played a part in the transition to peacetime when the war was finally over.

This life I led was not unusual for a G.P. of that era; in fact, the story of my family—the other Cleveland Browns—is representative of the stories of thousands of primary physicians who chose, as I did, to practice medicine in a rural or semi-rural setting. In villages and farm towns across America, these doctors loved and cared for their patients, took part in the affairs

FOREWORD

of their communities, forged links with the wider medical world, and raised families.

It was a demanding life—difficult, busy, often frantic—but one I wouldn't have exchanged for the world. Not long ago, I listened, intrigued, as a well-known cardio-thoracic surgeon told tales of his life. He talked of the hours he had spent in operating rooms, of the lives he had saved or prolonged, of the countless times he had neglected his family or cancelled social engagements at the last moment to respond to emergencies. But as I pondered his life, a little enviously, he turned to me and said, "You know, Marv, in medical school I always wanted to become a family doctor. But when I began my clinical and hospital training, I learned how difficult that kind of work is—so I took the easy way out and became a specialist. I believe the family physician has to be more knowledgeable than any other medical practitioner."

Certainly family practice demands a broad range of knowledge. I never knew what I would be facing: Would my next patient have an upper respiratory infection or a heart arrhythmia? A laceration that needed suturing or a strep throat? Would my patient be a child with Reye's Syndrome, a young man with venereal disease, or a diabetic needing a checkup? Would the problem be something I could treat on my own, or would I need a consultation?

But family practice demands more than broad knowledge. Unlike the specialist, the family doctor is not treating an ailment but a whole person. When a patient walked into my office, it was likely that not only had I treated her for years, but that I had treated her parents, her siblings, and her husband—and delivered her babies. The radio and television personality Paul Harvey summed it up when he recalled that in his day, babies were delivered, cared for through infancy, given their immunization shots and school physicals as children and their premarital blood tests as adults, treated for a variety of illnesses throughout their lives, and finally eased and comforted in the ailments of old age—all by the family doctor.

Those of us who started in primary care before World War II had to begin practicing medicine the hard way. With modern medicines, equipment, and techniques still being developed, our best tools in those early years were often sheer determination and dedication. We did try hard to keep up with new developments, however; pursuing our chosen field meant continuous, wide-ranging study. And over my lifetime, I saw a new world in medical care unfold. I lived—and practiced medicine—through the development of antibiotics and the polio vaccine. I watched as new methods of anesthesia, the establishment of blood banks, and the development of cardio-pulmonary bypass machines revolutionalized surgery, especially cardiac surgery. I saw the diagnosis and treatment of serious and complex conditions become quicker and more exact as technology created or refined X-ray imaging, CT scanning, sonography, and echo-cardiography. I saw the beginnings of organ transplants, lens implants, and chemotherapy.

I witnessed, too, the tremendous growth of specialty medicine and its effect on general practice. I lived through the formation of the American Academy of General Practice in 1947—and its transformation into the American Academy of Family Physicians in 1971. Despite—or perhaps because of—the explosion of specialty medical care, Americans have indicated clearly their desire for a doctor of their own: one who knows them intimately, who responds when they need help, who can advise them as whole human beings—the total primary physician. I have watched with pride the phenomenal growth of the AAFP in recent years, and the corresponding improvement in the training of family physicians, equipping them better than ever for the diagnosis and treatment of their patients' ills. I believe that, at present, the well-trained family physician with a three-year residency behind him can diagnose and treat efficiently 90 to 95 percent of the patients who come through his office door.

When I began practicing medicine in the late 1930s, the

FOREWORD

basic objective for all doctors was to preserve life; we fought constantly to overcome the limitations of our knowledge, techniques, and equipment to achieve this. As a solo practitioner in a rural area, where the nearest hospital was twenty miles away, I often had to improvise with the means at hand and to make snap decisions on life-and-death matters. Often I faced such crises under stress or in a state of exhaustion. Fortunately, most of the time I came up with the correct procedure. As I look back, however, I realize that there were times when my judgment could have been challenged. For these incidents, I apologize to any of my former patients; I always tried to do my best for them, and any errors of judgment I made were honest ones.

Toward the end of my practice, technological advances had greatly eased the processes of diagnosis and treatment. But the same advances have profoundly affected the purpose of medicine; the simple objective of preserving life that guided us in my early days has been replaced by complex questions about the nature of life and death and about the quality of life.

The delivery of patient care is also changing radically. Between 1965 and 1980 the number of medical schools has doubled, and some predict a surplus of physicians in the United States by 1990. The increasing competition resulting from this rise in the number of physicians is already affecting modes of medical practice. The house call—a procedure standard in my early years of practice and scorned later on—is once more in vogue. Home delivery, too, is making a comeback. And the need to cater to patient convenience has also generated a new phenomenon: walk-in medical offices which are springing up everywhere from shopping malls to converted gas stations.

All the changes don't alter one central fact, however. Patients will always need care, and physicians will always be there to provide it. Moreover, doctors' concern for their patients will undoubtedly bring many more medical firsts in the next forty-odd years. What advances would you predict?

One

Arrival

It was a clear brisk day in mid-April 1938. The trees and bushes were beginning to bud, and the air had the tantalizing scent of wet earth and growing things that always signals spring. But for Bee and me, driving west along Route 49 with the clear blue sky overhead, the day and the road held special promise. We were on our way to the village of Cleveland, New York, to look over a medical practice that might become the cornerstone of our future. As a young doctor of twenty-five, only two years out of medical school, I was looking forward to starting my first private practice. My wife Bee was hoping for a settled home.

The two-lane highway wove through hilly, wooded countryside, scattered with farms. I went slowly, both to prolong the pleasant drive and to ease the ride for Bee, who was five months pregnant with our first child. The road dipped and rose. Suddenly, cresting a hill at the junction with Route 13, we could see Oneida Lake shimmering below us.

"How lovely," said Bee. "Do you think this could be what we're looking for?"

"I hope so, " I answered. "I really do."

Soon we passed through the village of North Bay and were traveling along Oneida Lake's north shore. It was by now late afternoon, and the sun was descending in the western sky. The

HOUSE CALLS

beauty of the water glistening in the low light enthralled and excited us. We passed the tiny community of Jewell and were soon driving into Cleveland: down Lake Street, and along the lake shore. Finally, at the corner of Lake and West Streets, we found the house we had been looking for. The late sunshine picked out the white Cape Cod house.

As we parked, Dr. Melamed and his wife Helen came out to meet us. He was a short, stocky, athletic-looking man in his early thirties, very pleasant and hospitable. He and his wife showed us around their combination home and office with pride.

"I've been here six years," Dr. Melamed told us. "Helen and I want to move to Oneida so I can join my cousin, Dr. Freshman, in his practice, but we'll both miss Cleveland."

As he talked, explaining the details of his practice to me, Bee and I were inspecting the house carefully. It was three years old. It wasn't very big, having only two bedrooms. It needed storm windows and insulation. It also needed decorating. But it had a nice office and a small waiting room. It had a garage with an entrance into the kitchen. And it had a magnificent view of Oneida Lake from nearly every room.

Bee squeezed my hand. I could sense her excitement although she was trying to keep her face solemn. I was having trouble keeping a smile from sliding across my face myself. Still, I told myself sternly, we had to be practical. The Melameds were asking seventy-five hundred dollars for the house and practice. For Bee and me, that represented quite a mortgage on the future, even assuming that we would get a bank to loan us what we needed. I tried hard to keep my mind on what Dr. Melamed was telling me about the practice.

"It's a demanding practice," he said. "There aren't many doctors out here, and there's not a drugstore for miles. Sometimes getting through to the farms in the winter is a real chore; some of the roads are pretty bad. You'll be working under less-than-ideal conditions a lot of the time, without good backup. But you'll never be bored; I can almost guarantee it. And there are

ARRIVAL

some really fine people in Cleveland. And having the lake so near—well, we've really grown to love it. In many ways, Helen and I will hate to leave, but we have our reasons."

After a time, Bee and I took our leave and got in the car for the drive to Syracuse, where we were staying with relatives. Finally, we were free to talk—to share our excitement and hope.

"What do you think?" Bee asked carefully. "Is the practice what you want?"

"It sounds interesting," I admitted. "And the location is really great." I started to smile. "I like it, Bee. That lake . . ."

"I like the house," said Bee. "It needs work, but it would be fun to get it into shape. Oh, Marv! Do you think we could get it?"

The next few days were filled with talk. We talked with each other, with our families, with friends—and with the bank. In the end, our enthusiasm won out over our sparse funds. With the help of loans and a mortgage, we were able to buy the practice and the house. We arranged to move in in September, after our child was due.

Bee and I were already familiar with central New York. I had grown up in Syracuse, thirty miles from Cleveland, and Bee and I had met there. But this small village, nestled on the north shore of Oneida Lake, would be a far cry from city life. And a rural practice would be a big change from the two hospital internships I had held.

I had graduated from the Syracuse College of Medicine, cum laude, in June 1936, one of a class of forty-six. I spent the following year as a rotating intern at the Syracuse General Hospital, which was then a small hospital of sixty beds. Two other interns were there at the same time, and among us we took part in all the medical procedures practiced there: internal medicine, surgery, obstetrics, pediatrics, and even laboratory work.

I learned a lot that year. One of my most vivid memories is of my first Caesarean section. The chief of obstetrics casually

15

asked me one day, "Marv, how would you like to do the section tomorrow?" With considerable trepidation, I said yes. The next morning I scrubbed up and donned my surgical mask and suit. With the help of a fellow intern, I performed a very successful classic Caesarean section. I delivered a beautiful seven-pound baby, and the mother recovered well enough to be discharged in two weeks, which was then the usual stay after a C-section. My pleasure and relief probably equaled the mother's own!

Another obstetrical case that first year didn't end so happily, however. I was on duty late one night when a local doctor called to say that he was sending in a woman he assumed was close to delivery. How right he was! The woman arrived shortly afterward and was immediately taken to the delivery room. She was a Gravida 8 Para 7, which means she was pregnant for the eighth time with seven children "at home." I was barely able to get my surgical gloves on before she delivered her baby spontaneously in breach position. The baby was fine, but immediately after delivery the mother went into deep shock. I started an intravenous saline infusion—we had no blood ready in those days—but she died within a few minutes.

My feelings can be imagined. Here I was, a twenty-four-year-old intern recently out of medical school, faced with telling a hopeful husband and father that his wife had died. I managed to do so, but the case was a sobering experience. It brought home to me that medicine is not all honey and roses, and that part of a doctor's duty is to console the families of those who die.

I obtained a partial autopsy of this patient and studied the uterus that was removed. It showed a large hole, and through this rupture ran many grayish ropey growths, or villi, some even attached to the lower bowels. The woman had had a *placenta percreta*, a severe and rare complication. The placenta, through which a growing fetus gets its nutrients, usually detaches from the walls of the uterus easily after the baby is born. In this case, however, the soft, spongy layer of the placenta was entirely absent, and the villi were stuck to the uterus and had even grown through the uterine walls. As labor progressed, the thinning uterine wall gave way causing severe shock, hemorrhage, and death.

This condition of *placenta percreta* is very rare; indeed, according to a 1976 study by Dr. Nicholas J. Teteris of Ohio State University, only thirty-seven cases have been recorded through 1970. Today, with adequate prenatal care and sonography, this kind of tragedy is preventable. The lesson it taught me, however, is one all doctors learn in time.

During my year at the old General, I was given room, board, and ten dollars a month for my services. I spent most of the money on taxi fares so that I could spend time with Bee, then my fiancée, who lived some distance away. The hospital gave me the last ten days of my internship off so that we could marry and have a honeymoon before I began my next appointment.

Although it was receding somewhat, the Great Depression was not yet over; a fancy wedding was out of the question. So on June 20, 1937, our small wedding was held in the study of Rabbi Benjamin Friedman at the Temple Society of Concord in Syracuse. There Beatrice Gertrude Lucasen became my wife. She was the most radiant and beautiful bride I have ever seen, and our love for each other flourished unabated until the day she died.

Only our families and a few close friends attended the ceremony. Afterward, we had a family luncheon at the Hotel Syracuse and a simple reception at the Lucasens' home. Finally, Bee and I slipped out the back door, went across lots, and were driven to Canastota to catch the Albany train. From there we traveled to the Adirondack Mountains for a week-long honeymoon.

The trip was wonderful, but all too soon we were back in Syracuse packing for a move to Ogdensburg, New York, where I had taken an appointment as a medical intern at the St. Lawrence State Hospital, a mental institution. This time I was paid a stipend

17

of eighteen hundred dollars for the year. We were also provided with a small furnished apartment in a staff home, some food, local telephone service, and a cleaning woman once a week.

We remained in Ogdensburg for thirteen months. I did the physical examinations and psychiatric screening on most of the new admissions to St. Lawrence. I was also in charge of the sick ward, treating any patients who came down with the ordinary organic illnesses we are all prone to. And a new patient was assigned to me every week for a psychiatric workup that was later evaluated at a staff conference.

Twice a week I had to make the rounds of the outlying buildings, generally in the evenings. Most of the time, these rounds were interesting and informative. But in the winter, when cold winds and heavy snows seemed to flow down the St. Lawrence River from Canada, I heartily wished they could be cancelled. I often remember those dark, lonely excursions, trudging through deep snow drifts in the wind and cold.

Staff members were given keys to all the buildings and to the individual wards. We had to lock each door behind us as we passed through. Today, most mental hospitals have an open-door policy; patients are controlled through a variety of very specific drugs instead of through locks. But in the 1930s, medications for mental patients were very few. Large doses of chloral hydrate together with bromides were standard methods of sedating patients when necessary. Paraldehyde injections were also routine for excitable patients.

St. Lawrence State Hospital was the first hospital in the state system to use shock treatment. The process had been pioneered by doctors in Eastern Europe, who had found that convulsions produced by an intravenous injection of Metrazol could improve the mental condition of some patients. Since St. Lawrence State Hospital was in a remote area of northern New York, where publicity could be kept to a minimum, the state mental hygiene director decided that it would be an ideal place to introduce shock treatment experimentally. I was in charge

ARRIVAL

of the sick ward and had had more experience in giving drugs intravenously than the other members of the staff, so I was elected to give the convulsive therapy. We studied up on the work done in Europe. Then a young male schizophrenic patient was chosen to receive the drug.

Nurses, staff doctors, even a motion picture camera crew gathered to watch the treatment. I drew 3 ml. of Metrazol into a syringe and injected it very slowly into the patient. When 2 ml. had been injected, he began to have classic convulsive seizures. I withdrew the syringe quickly, and, with nurses and doctors at his bedside, the patient continued to jerk his head and limbs for about two minutes. Then he settled into a deep sleep, lasting about ten minutes, after which he slowly became aware of his surroundings. For reasons I never discovered, St. Lawrence State Hospital never repeated this experiment with Metrazol, with this or any other patient, although this patient seemed to improve temporarily. However, we did use other methods to induce seizures: first, intramuscular injections of camphor in oil, then insulin shock, and finally electroshock, a treatment still in use today.

The experience I got at St. Lawrence State Hospital was very valuable to me later. I would recommend some psychiatric background for anyone going into family practice. Familiarity with mental disorders helped me to determine when an illness in my patients had a mental, rather than a physical, cause. Often, when I encountered psychosomatic ailments, I treated them very successfully with placebos. But when a patient had a more serious mental or emotional problem, my St. Lawrence training enabled me to recognize this and recommend treatment by an appropriate specialist.

One of the bonuses of life in Ogdensburg was that Bee and I had quite a lot of leisure time. My work hours were from 9:00 A.M. to 4:30 P.M. with an hour for lunch. This light schedule allowed us to visit friends and relatives and see plenty of each other; looking back, that time seems almost an extension of

HOUSE CALLS

our honeymoon. We had other young people to socialize with, and I even organized a hospital basketball team. The staff people were for the most part young and energetic like ourselves. We found friendships with some of them that are still going strong.

There were drawbacks, too, however. All staff members were under the tutelage of the hospital director, Dr. Taddiken. He was a great teacher at our staff conferences, but he was also very stern and stuck to the letter of the law. Thus when a friend visiting from Syracuse ended up staying the night, I was called into Dr. Taddiken's office the next day to identify him, give the reason for his visit, and explain why I hadn't asked permission for his overnight stay. Another time, Bee and I moved some furniture from one wall to another in our small apartment. The cleaning woman reported this breach of the rules, and once again I was called on the carpet for not asking permission.

These intrusions into our private life made a deep impression on Bee and me. We decided to look for a general practice in a small town partly to get away from this feeling of having someone constantly looking over our shoulders.

There were other reasons for our decision, too. In the 1930s, most doctors began as generalists. It was common for a doctor to practice general medicine for a few years, save enough money to keep him going for two or three years while he learned a specialty, and then open his office in that field. I wanted to go into general practice for its own sake, however. I saw it as a field full of interest and variety, in which I would continue to learn throughout my life. Bee and I had also decided that we wanted to settle in a small town yet close enough to a city so that we could take advantage of its cultural and social resources. If possible, I also wanted to be near a medical center.

During the winter of 1937-38 we discovered to our joy that Bee was pregnant. We both hoped to have our future settled by the time the baby arrived. We looked at several practices in northern New York, but none appealed to us. Then in April 1938 I came to Syracuse to pick up a new Plymouth—a major

ARRIVAL

investment at 750 dollars. While there, I looked into a practice in Meridian, New York, a few miles away. It was a strictly rural practice involving many house calls, home deliveries, and office work, with the usual communicable diseases thrown in. In those days, these included not only measles, mumps, chicken pox, and rubella, but also whooping cough and polio. The practice looked challenging, and I planned to discuss it with Bee when I got back to Ogdensburg. I visited the doctor selling the practice and then went to see a lawyer to learn what would be involved if we did go to Meridian. As I left his office on the fourth floor of the Seitz Building in Syracuse, I found I'd just missed the elevator and decided to walk down. On the third floor stairs I almost bumped into Edmund Port, a lawyer and old family friend who had his office in the same building. We exchanged greetings, and I told him the reason for my visit to the building.

"What do you want to go to Meridian for?" Ed asked.
"My good friend Marty Melamed has a hellava setup in Cleveland, and he wants to sell out."

"Where's Cleveland?" I asked.

After some discussion, Ed called Dr. Melamed and made an appointment for Beatrice and me to visit him in two weeks. Our visit convinced us that Cleveland was just what we had been looking for: a rural practice with plenty of variety yet within reach of the city of Syracuse; a solo practice yet with access to hospitals in Oneida and Syracuse; and a house set in beautiful countryside next to a lovely lake. A quirk of a quick elevator had given us a home and practice that would dominate our lives for almost forty-five years. I brought to it a mixture of old-fashioned medicine, dedication, energy, and hope.

Two
Settling In

Beatrice and I decided to leave Ogdensburg on August 1, 1938, so that she could await the arrival of our child at her parents' home in Syracuse. I would spend the month of August with the Melameds learning my new practice.

I had been given a trial run in Cleveland before August when Dr. Melamed had asked me to cover him for a few days in June while he and his wife took a short vacation. I was able to get the time off from St. Lawrence State Hospital, and Bee accompanied me. My first home delivery took place during this stay. I got a call from the local baby nurse, Mrs. Bopp, saying that a Mrs. Max Whipple was in labor at the Bopp house, where the delivery was to take place. I drove right over. Mrs. Bopp, a self-taught health aide, was a large, big-bosomed woman with a ruddy complexion. She was always warm and confident, exuding friendliness and comfort. But her medical ideas were a curious hangover from her Swiss homeland. As she got things ready for Mrs. Whipple's delivery, she told me that she had "shterilized" the sheets by placing them between newpapers and heating them in the oven! Despite such odd ideas, Mrs. Bopp helped me to deliver a perfect baby girl. The Whipples named her Beatrice, after my wife.

After this experience I was more eager than ever to get going.

HOUSE CALLS

Finally, on the first of August, I delivered Bee to her parents' home in Syracuse and the next day went on to Cleveland. There, with Dr. Melamed coaching, I began to learn the practice that would be mine alone. It was soon clear to me that I would be a busy man. Besides office work, minor surgery, house calls, home deliveries, conducting immunization clinics, and assisting at major surgeries, the practice involved acting as health officer, coroner's physician, school doctor, and summer camp physician.

On August 13, at six in the morning, I was awakened by the telephone. I answered, and the voice at the other end said, "Honey, I'm having five minute labor pains. What will I do?"

"Who's this?" I asked.

"Who else calls you 'honey'?" asked Bee.

Instantly I was wide awake. I told Bee to go to the hospital, and I was soon on my way to Syracuse. Later that day our son Neal was ushered into the world. He was the most beautiful baby we had ever seen. I spent the rest of August driving back and forth from Cleveland to Syracuse daily, so as to spend as much time as possible with Bee and Neal. By the end of August, Bee was recovered enough to make the move to Cleveland. On September 1, we all came to the Cape Cod house in Cleveland for good. Finally I had my wife, my two-week-old son, and my own medical practice together in one place.

At the beginning, it seemed a good thing that our house was rather small; we didn't have much to put in it. Bee's parents, who moved in with us that first year to give us a hand, brought their furniture for the living room and their bedroom. I bought, on credit, a pair of large lounge chairs that went nicely on either side of the fireplace. Bee and I slept on a box spring and a mattress on the floor until our bedroom furniture arrived. I was getting it wholesale from my brother, Ben, who was in the furniture business, but even so it was six months before it arrived. My sister, Fannie, kindly contributed a crib for Neal.

My office was also sparsely furnished. I had a desk and two chairs, an old steel examining table, a steel stool, a medicine cabinet, and another small cabinet containing my few instruments. The tiny waiting room had six chairs. There was a small closet with shelves for medicines and a water closet squeezed in.

On the wall in my office I hung my B.A. diploma and the New York State certificate qualifying me to practice medicine and surgery. But my M.D. diploma was missing. I still owed tuition money to the Syracuse College of Medicine, so my diploma was withheld until this bill was paid. It was three years before I hung my M.D. diploma on the wall. It was a proud moment when I was finally able to do so.

While Bee was getting the house in shape, I was plunging into my practice. My office hours were from 1:00 to 3:00 and 7:00 to 8:00 P.M. every day except Thursdays and Sundays. Often the afternoon hours stretched to 5:00 P.M. and the evening hours to 10:00 P.M. Then there were house calls in the mornings, between office hours, and often well into the night. I also delivered babies at home and in the Oneida City Hospital, and even in the old St. Mary's Hospital in Syracuse. As if all this wasn't enough, I had my duties as school doctor, health officer, and coroner's physician.

My very first patient was Mrs. Cora Eaton. Her husband, Arthur, a rural mail carrier, had recently retired. She had fallen and hurt her knee; when it hadn't gotten better after two days, she called me. I examined her at her home, treated her, and asked for my fee of $2.50. My practice had begun!

On my way to and from the Eatons' house, I would normally have passed the home of Clinton Drum, the village mayor. That day, however, the streets around his home were blocked off so that I had to make a detour. It turned out that Mr. Drum had suffered a heart attack several days earlier, and the streets were blocked off so that traffic would not disturb his rest. How often would such courtesy be practiced now, I wonder?

At the beginning of my practice I decided to keep the same fee schedule that Dr. Melamed had had. I charged $1.50 for an office visit. That fee included pills and certain tests like

HOUSE CALLS

urinalyses, and often I would treat a second or third family member at no extra charge. The full charge for a house call was $2.50. If my patient lived beyond the Cleveland village limits, I added a charge of twenty-five cents a mile to the fee. My fee for delivering a baby was $35, and for a circumcision, $5. I took care of simple fractures, removed small tumors, incised boils, and stitched up wounds for fees in line with those above.

For the first three years Bee worked with me as my only office help. She answered the telephone, held children for suturing, held limbs while I put on plaster casts, and held babies while I performed circumcisions. She did all these things between her own chores: running a house, taking care of our new baby, shopping, participating in local organizations, and trying to keep me happy. Despite all she had to do, it seemed that Bee was always at my side, her laughter filling the air, giving me aid, comfort, and encouragement when I most needed them. She was the catalyst in our close-knit family. After a good night's sleep—when I could get it—I always looked forward to spending at least some part of the day with her.

Bee's parents, Miner and Harriet Lucasen, were also a great help that first year. Her mother, especially, helped out whenever needed by babysitting and cooking. Bee and I have always been very grateful for their support in those early, busy days.

In addition to our home and practice, Bee and I were busy learning about our new community. In its heyday at the turn of the century, Cleveland had been a thriving village of nearly twenty-five hundred people. Its fortunes were built on sand: the finest grade of silica sand used in making window glass. One by one, however, Cleveland's glass factories closed down. The village dwindled until, by the time Bee and I arrived in 1938, the population was only about nine hundred. It was now a quiet, rather sleepy community. Life went along there at a slow pace. There were small vegetable gardens in most of the yards and very often a family cow.

Most of Cleveland's citizens were middle-aged to old, with

only a few growing families to liven things up. Many of the people were retired, some were salespersons, and others were commuters living in Cleveland and working in larger communities nearby. Most of our neighbors and patients had middle or low-middle incomes, but they were hard-working and scrupulous about paying their bills.

As we settled in, Bee and I made many friends among them. One of the first we meet was old Jim Gallagher. At the age of ninety-one, he was still as sharp as a tack. A distinguished lawyer, over the years he had also become a political leader on the North Shore. During our first week in Cleveland, he dropped in to my office, not for medical treatment, but for a chat. He welcomed me to Cleveland and gave me some valuable pointers about life in the area. On that first visit, he also talked me into subscribing to the *National Geographic* magazine, a subscription that I have kept up ever since and that has provided me with much pleasure.

Another visitor that first week was Eugene Dawley. Gene was a jolly, expansive man who ran a fish market out of a barn at the back of his house. He was also the poormaster for the township of Constantia, which included Cleveland. In 1938 there was no welfare system, no Medicare, no Medicaid. But since there were many poor families in the area, we had instead a local poormaster.

"Doc," he told me, "there are a lot of people who need medical attention but can't pay for it. I know who they are, and when you or I get a call from one of these people, I'll go with you at first so you know your way around. Keep track of your calls, and at the end of the month give me the list and your fees and I'll give you a check."

Those trips with Gene were an education. He knew which people were truly poor and which were the malingerers, and he made sure I did too. Many of these people also came to my office for treatment. When they did, I would often treat the whole family for the same $1.50 fee.

HOUSE CALLS

I kept careful track for Gene of my calls and fees, and each month he would give me a check. On average, he paid me $75 a month for treating the poor patients. After a few months, Gene would call me up to ask what the total for the previous month amounted to, without even asking me for my list.

I often wish that we still had poormasters today instead of our centralized assistance programs. Gene knew the people he represented; he knew their incomes, their lifestyles, who their parents were, how they came to be down on their luck. And he made sure they had medical care when they needed it.

Two of the people who helped us the most in those early days were Ken and Molly Godfrey. Both were large-built, friendly, and easygoing; Ken, especially, seemed to wear a perpetual grin. He was a sort of jack-of-all-trades in the area, and Molly was a cleaning woman. They supplemented their income by selling vegetables from their large garden and fish which they caught by ice-fishing on Oneida Lake in the winter. They were also caretakers for several lakeshore cottages.

They both worked for us when we were starting out, and they were both hard workers. Ken kept our lawn mowed with an old hand mower. I paid him fifty cents a time. That doesn't seem like much money now, but the Great Depression was still on then, and Ken was glad to get the money. Molly helped Bee in the house. I can still hear her loud voice as she hollered from upstairs, "Hey, Bee, what'll I put on this kid?" or "Bee, where's the erl for the terlet?" Molly had a Brooklyn accent that never left her.

Bee took great comfort in Molly in another way. Molly was the only other Jewish woman in the area. Later, they became Eastern Star Sisters together. Many times Bee and I would join Ken and Molly at either Eastern Star or Masonic covered-dish suppers.

Two of the most colorful characters we met in those early days, however, were the Reverend George MacNish and Father John Butler. Both became very good friends of ours.

SETTLING IN

The Reverend Mac, as he was known, served for thirty years as the rector of the St. James Episcopal Church in Cleveland and also of the Trinity Church in Constantia. When I first saw him, he was loping slowly up the hill on the second hole of the nine-hole Cleveland Golf Course, his white hair ruffling in the breeze and a full golf bag slung over one shoulder. When he reached the crest of the hill he stopped, and I was introduced to him. He looked me over carefully. I have wondered what he thought of me at that first meeting. He certainly made a lasting impression on me: a cigarette dangled between his lips and the ashes fell over his chest every so often. He had a tall, athletic body and a face made striking by deep brown eyes and bushy white eyebrows.

I next saw Mac at the three-day Firemen's Field Days at Constantia. A parade opened the event. At its head, dressed in his World War I uniform and riding high on a glossy brown horse, was Mac. He loved parades; I later found out that he led the Constantia parade every year.

A few days later, I saw him again. This time, he was riding the waves on Oneida Lake in his one-man racing scull. As I got to know him, I realized that these three occasions were typical; Mac's interests were wide-ranging and his zest for life insatiable.

Despite the fact that we were not members of his congregation, Mac kindly invited us to several church suppers at his house. His home was almost as impressive as he was. It stood on a high bluff at the eastern edge of the village, overlooking the lake. It had a thirty-foot living room with a huge vaulted ceiling upheld by hand-hewn beams that Mac had dragged himself from a ruined barn nearby. There was certainly plenty of room for a supper party.

I remember waiting at the first one we attended for Mac to say grace. Everyone was seated, ready to eat, except Mac. There was a solemn pause. Then Mac lowered himself into his chair, saying as he did so, "Good food, good meat; Oh Hell, let's eat!" The room exploded with laughter.

HOUSE CALLS

Mac's lively taste in graces didn't mean that he didn't have a serious side. He was highly intelligent, very well read, and interested in everything. Over his life, he corresponded with the Archbishop of Canterbury, President Theodore Roosevelt, and General George Patton, under whom he had served in World War I. He wrote two books, in the latter quoting, among others, Plato, Socrates, and Darwin. Mac's style was captured in a 1949 column by Joe Beamish in the *Syracuse Herald Journal*: "During his final years, he was ravaged by cancer. Yet he continued to preach, often clutching the altar rail to hold himself up. One such sermon began, 'The atom'll get you if you don't watch out!' Another time, he told his congregation, 'One of God's greatest gifts to man is his friends. I thank him for mine.' That was the whole sermon as he could say no more. I'm sure that Mac's friends echoed that sentiment."

Father John Butler had come to Cleveland shortly before Bee and I did. He was the Catholic priest for St. Mary's Church in Cleveland and also conducted Masses at the Catholic church in nearby Sylvan Beach. He was in his mid-fifties when we met him, a round-faced man with very blue eyes and sparse graying hair, whose strong Irish brogue delighted us. Village rumor held that, despite his age, Father Butler was new to the priesthood; apparently he had been an accountant in New York City until his mid-forties.

Since the church and rectory stood at the other end of the short block from our house, we soon became friends. Father Butler was a kind man, well-liked by his parishoners and by most other people too. He was very stern with children, however, and at times this caused rumblings among his parishoners.

During our first year in Cleveland, Father Butler came to our home frequently to play bridge with Bee and her parents. Often the Reverend MacNish would also join these games. These sessions often proved very lively; both churchmen played a mean game of bridge. Often as I sat in my office, I could hear voices from the living room raised in excited but friendly argument.

Near the beginning of our acquaintance, Father Butler gave

me a good scare. Each summer, when the hundreds of vacationers visiting the lake meant that more church Masses were needed, Father Butler was sent an assistant. That first June, the assistant was a young, newly-ordained priest from Syracuse. One night about midnight, this fledgling priest called me in a panic.

"Dr. Brown, you must come at once. Father Butler is vomiting blood, and I don't know what to do! Please come right now."

I pulled on my clothes, grabbed my bag, and was at Father Butler's bedside in minutes. The sight that greeted me was shocking, even to a doctor. Blood was everywhere: on the sheets, blankets, floor, and walls. My first impression was that I had a critical patient on my hands.

When I examined him, it became clear that the priest was bleeding from an upper intestinal lesion; I could only hope that the blood was coming from a stomach ulcer rather than from a cancerous growth. I immediately gave him a dose of morphine and had the young priest get cracked ice to put in Father Butler's mouth. He had already lost so much blood, however, that I really believed he was dying. So I asked him if he wished for the last rites of the Catholic church.

"Please, if you would," he answered.

The young priest was so shocked and frightened that he seemed almost unable to function. With the prodding of a Jewish doctor, however, he finally gathered together the holy water and other articles needed to perform the last rites.

"I'll take care of the feet," I told him, "but you have to do the rest."

With that, he pulled himself together, and between us we muddled through. When the last rites were concluded, I was rewarded by the look of peace on Father Butler's face.

Once the religious imperative had been taken care of, medical necessity took priority once again. We loaded Father Butler into my home-made ambulance and before long had deposited him at St. Joseph's Hospital in Syracuse. Tests there confirmed a diagnosis of duodenal ulcer. After several whole blood transfusions and supportive treatment, the bleeding stopped. Father Butler slowly recovered. With the help of a special diet, he was able to keep his ulcer under control and was soon back in our living room, winning more games of bridge.

Father Butler and Reverend Mac livened our days and broadened our outlook—as we did theirs—for several of our early years in Cleveland. Their friendships were among Cleveland's many gifts to us.

Three
A Hard Day's Night

It was on June 15, 1939, that the full enormity of what I'd taken on was brought home to me. That day at 6:30 A.M. someone began knocking at my office door, which was just below our bedroom. It was Mr. Lester Tyler, whose family lived in the village on Clay Street.

"Sorry to wake you, Doc," he said, "but my wife's gone into labor. Can you come right away?"

I dressed hurriedly, grabbed my O.B. bag, and was at the Tylers' home about ten minutes later. While Mr. Tyler waited anxiously, I examined his wife. "Don't worry," I said. "Everything's going fine. It's likely to be a few hours, though, so I'm going back to the office. Call me when your pains are five minutes apart."

I drove home, looking forward to a nice breakfast with Bee before starting work in the office. I had barely reached home, however, when the phone rang.

"Dr. Brown, I'm Mrs. Howe's neighbor—you know, in Constantia Center? Mrs. Howe's started labor, and I think you ought to get over here as soon as you can."

Sighing, I set out once again. Upon examining Mrs. Howe, I found that she, too, was progressing slowly. I told her neighbor, who fortunately had a telephone, to keep me informed of her

33

HOUSE CALLS

progress.

I was just getting into my car to return home when Mr. Corsette from North Constantia drove up and hailed me. He had heard I was at the Howes' and had driven there to find me.

"Dr. Brown, you've got to come right away. My wife's in labor."

Thinking longingly of my breakfast, I followed him along the back way to North Constantia, trying to avoid the potholes in the dirt roads. When we reached their simple wooden house I went in and found that, like the others, Mrs. Corsette's labor would take some time. Finally I was able to head home for breakfast.

As I drove, I considered the situation. I had three women in labor, each progressing slowly. Mrs. Howe's home was six miles from Mrs. Tyler's, and Mrs. Corsette's was four miles farther. Only one of the women, Mrs. Howe, could be reached by telephone. I had one set of instruments, a gallon of lysol solution for sterilization, sterile rubber gloves, and no professional help. I could see it was going to be an interesting day.

Things began to happen about noon. My telephone rang, and Mrs. Howe's neighbor reported that Mrs. Howe was having hard pains. I drove there only to find that Mrs. Howe's pains had slowed up again. The baby's head was coming down, however—a sign of progress. I had been there about an hour, waiting for the pains to pick up again, when Mr. Corsette appeared.

"Dr. Brown, my wife's pains are getting closer together. I think it will be time soon. You've got to come now!"

I couldn't leave Mrs. Howe, however, with an apparent inertia of the uterus, since the baby's head was now well down in the birth canal and she was fully dilated. I decided to deliver the baby with a low forceps application. Forceps were necessary since the muscular power of the uterus seemed insufficient to push the baby out.

I boiled up my forceps in a large roasting pan from the Howe's kitchen. Then I taught Mrs. Howe's neighbor how to drop ether on an open mask. I put on my sterile gloves, sterilized Mrs. Howe with lysol solution, and delivered a beautiful baby girl, who cried loudly as soon as she emerged. Quickly I checked the baby, tied the umbilical cord, and expressed the placenta. I told the neighbor how to massage Mrs. Howe's lower abdomen. Then I cleaned my instruments, tossed them in my bag, jumped in the car, and drove as fast as I could over the dirt roads to the Corsette home, four miles away.

I arrived to find Mr. Corsette practically dancing with impatience. This baby was not the Corsettes' first, so he could tell that the birth was imminent.

"Please hurry, Dr. Brown," he urged. "The baby's almost here." He was quite right. I didn't have time to examine Mrs. Corsette because by the time I had applied the ever-ready lysol solution and put on my sterile gloves I could see the head. Two more contractions did it. The Corsettes were the parents of a fine baby boy, who also cried lustily.

I checked the baby, cleaned up, made sure that Mrs. Corsette was in good shape, and then headed back to the Howes' to make sure that she and her baby were comfortable. The neighbor had done a good job, and everything was in good order. I was just about to drive home, however, when Mrs. Howe's neighbor ran out to tell me that Bee had called. Mrs. Tyler was ready to deliver.

Once again I set off at top speed, although trying to hurry along the narrow and curving Panther Lake Road was not easy. However, after four miles, I hit Route 49; then I could make good time. Soon I was back in Cleveland, at Mrs. Tyler's bedside.

Once again, birth was not far away. After only twenty minutes, I delivered another crying baby girl. I checked her and found her perfect. Then I tied the cord, expressed the placenta, checked for excess bleeding, cleaned my instruments, gave instructions and prescribed medication to keep the uterus firm, and finally drove home.

That evening I did some serious thinking about my practice. The practicing physicians nearest to me were at Central Square, fifteen miles to the west; Camden, twelve miles to the north; Rome, twenty-five miles to the east; and Oneida, twenty miles to the southeast. A doctor did live in Sylvan Beach, ten miles away at the eastern end of Oneida Lake, but he was old, and his practice was winding down. The nearest hospitals available to my patients were in Oneida and Rome and in Syracuse, thirty-two miles distant. There was no ambulance service available except for that provided by undertakers in Parish, Rome, Central Square, and Oneida. For the most part, in emergencies, I would have only myself to rely on. Could I handle so much responsibility?

My mind began to go back over the day's events. Despite the distances, I had delivered three fine babies. With the help of my patients' families, their neighbors, and my own wife, I had kept track of the mothers' progress and managed to be with each patient when I was needed most. I had helped to bring about the miracle of birth three times in one day. The responsibilities were scary. But the rewards were terrific. It was worth it, I decided. It was definitely worth it.

My resolve was tested many times in the years that followed. The demands on my time and energy often left little to spare for my own growing family or for our friends. Moreover, much of this time and energy was being expended, not in the direct practice of my profession, but in getting to my patients or in trying to communicate with them. Like Mrs. Corsette, many of my patients didn't have telephones; many lived far out of town and could be reached only by dirt roads which turned into swamps in spring and were often blocked by deep snowdrifts in winter. Weather often seemed a partner in my practice, smoothing the way and lending pleasure to my work in the warm summer months, yet hindering it terribly in wet or winter seasons.

Many of my most taxing cases seemed to take place during,

A HARD DAY'S NIGHT

or just after, bitter snowstorms. The winter of 1947-48 was especially severe. It snowed and snowed and then snowed some more, leaving many patients who lived on farms more or less housebound.

One week, after a series of snowstorms, I got a number of calls from such housebound patients. But if they couldn't get out of their homes by car, neither could I get in; I had to resort to older methods of transport. I contacted Glenn Marsh, a farmer who lived just west of Cleveland, and asked him to take me on my rounds. Soon he was at my office door—in a "two-horse open sleigh"! Carrying a pair of snowshoes I had borrowed from my neighbor, Herbert Oatman, I climbed into the sleigh, and we were off. Since the temperature was below freezing, the day proved to be very invigorating! The people I treated appreciated my visits, however, and I appreciated Glenn's help.

That day was only one of several occasions when I did my rounds by sleigh and snowshoe. In the first years of my practice, I drafted another neighbor, Willis Tyler, to drive me in his sleigh; in the late forties, Glenn Marsh often took me. The aid given one another by people on the North Shore was one of the things about country life that Bee and I most enjoyed and admired. In a crisis, everyone pitched in and helped.

I remember another occasion, the winter before, when a whole crew of people turned out to help one of my patients. Mrs. Frank Spoon was due to deliver a baby that March, and the snowstorms were far from over. The Spoons ran a farm several miles beyond Panther Lake on a dirt road. Just before the approach to their house, the road dipped into a deep ravine. In addition, Mrs. Spoon was a diabetic; I had had a rather difficult time managing her pregnancy. Therefore, when I got a call on the evening of March 8, informing me that her labor pains had started, I hurried right out, taking Hoopey, my helper, with me.

It had been snowing hard for two days; and I wondered if Hoopey and I would make it through the ravine. But as we

37

HOUSE CALLS

approached, I could see many lighted lanterns through the swirling snow, and, by their glow, as many as twenty men shoveling snow as fast as they could. It was difficult to operate a tractor in the snow-filled ravine, and so the Spoons' neighbors had turned out to clear it by hand. The work was backbreaking, but the crew of volunteers soon accomplished it, and I was able to reach the house.

In the event, Mrs. Spoon's pains subsided, indicating false labor. I was disturbed to find, however, that I couldn't locate any fetal heart sounds. I told the Spoons of this and tried to prepare them for trouble; three days later I returned to deliver a stillborn fetus. It was a tragic outcome, but for me that tragedy was redeemed a little at least by the generous help of the Spoons' friends and neighbors, who had done all they could to give the expected baby a chance.

I remember a night a few years earlier—in January 1943—when similar help saved my own life. I had been called to the home of Mrs. Grace License, a patient I had inherited from Dr. Melamed. Mrs. License had advanced pulmonary tuberculosis, and I had been treating her for some time. Back then there were no specific medicines for tuberculosis: Treatment consisted of seeing that the patient was provided with rest, nutritious meals, fresh air, and good care. Despite this regimen, Mrs. License's condition had been deteriorating for some time. That January night, Mr. License called me a little after 8:00 P.M. to tell me his wife had died. He asked me to come and pronounce her dead and to notify the undertaker.

That night Bee was out playing bridge about a half mile away. I looked outside and found that the snow which had been falling for some time was now coming down fast and furiously and that the temperature, too, was going down. There were only four inches of snow on the ground as yet, however, so I settled for rubbers and my short coat for the mile-and-a-half trip. I told the babysitter where I was going and said I'd be back in about half an hour.

A HARD DAY'S NIGHT

I reached the Licenses' about 8:30, and pronounced Mrs. License dead. I called the undertaker, comforted the family as best I could, and then left to return home. The Licenses lived off Route 49, about a mile and a half west of Cleveland, on the Panther Lake Road. I drove down the Panther Lake Road all right, and turned east toward Cleveland on Route 49, but I had gone barely an eighth of a mile when I hit a snowdrift about four feet deep. I tried to move the car, but it was stuck fast. Then I tried to get out, but the car was embedded in such a way that the doors wouldn't open. I decided to stay in the car with the lights on, hoping that someone in the house on a hill nearby would see me and come down to help me. I was directly under a street light.

Time passed. No one came. Nine forty-five passed, then 10:00, then 10:30. I kept the car heater on and the lights blinking. The wind and snow were getting steadily worse; the temperature continued to drop. I was told afterward that the temperature was ten degrees below zero, with a wind-chill factor of forty to fifty degrees below zero.

At 11:00 P.M. the heater went off. I huddled up the best I could and waited for help.

In the meantime, Bee's bridge game had broken up early because of the weather. When Bee got home, the babysitter told her where I had gone and when I had said I would be back. Bee correctly guessed that I was stuck in a snowdrift. She called the Licenses and was told that I had left well over an hour before.

Bee decided that I probably needed help. She called Harold Morse, one of Cleveland's leading citizens, who ran a garage in the village.

"Harold, Marv went out to the Licenses' and started back over an hour ago. I'm afraid he's run into trouble. Can you find him for me?"

Harold Morse could always be counted on in an emergency. He was soon heading toward the Licenses with a truck. He was

HOUSE CALLS

back again almost immediately, however. Even with a truck, the heavy snow and gusting winds were too much; he'd had to turn back. Harold then called up Kenneth Godfrey, our handyman, who could also be counted on for help in any emergency.

Soon the two of them had headed out again—but again the storm turned them back. Still more help was needed, so they drafted Robert Landgraff and Al and Herb Ransom. This time, all five men set off in Harold's truck. Two more times the storm turned them back. Each time they reappeared in our driveway Bee's heart sank a little farther.

Finally, they tried a new approach. They drove as far as they could. Then each man tied a stout rope around his waist, and began searching on foot, armed with a flashlight that each man cast in a different direction. In this manner, wading through the drifting snow and fighting the bitter winds, they finally spotted me.

By this time it was 1:30 A.M. I had fallen asleep. The next thing I knew, someone was tapping on the car window and shining a flashlight on my face. It was Harold. He shoveled me out, and, using the rope, guided me back to his truck. The six of us crowded in and were soon pulling into my driveway.

When I walked into the living room Bee burst into tears and threw her arms around me.

"What's all this fuss?" I asked her. "I feel great. But just think, Bee, you've missed your chance. Just a week ago I took out an extra $10,000 life insurance policy. You could have been a rich widow!"

If I have managed to describe my wife at all, you can imagine her response. I wasn't sure I was going to survive the night after all.

The night I almost fell asleep for good in my car was certainly a night to remember, but the weather was usually more of a threat to my patients than to me. I remember another case that occurred in a bitter snowstorm that ended very tragically.

A HARD DAY'S NIGHT

It was about 5:30 P.M. on St. Valentine's Day, and it had been snowing steadily since morning. A frantic husband called and told me that his wife had suddenly collapsed to the floor. She was having trouble breathing, so the husband (who fortunately was a Boy Scout leader) and a friend had been taking turns giving her mouth-to-mouth resuscitation. I told him to continue until I got there, and then headed out the door.

By this time, the snow was coming down fast, and the drive to the woman's home in North Bay, which usually took about ten minutes, took thirty instead. When I entered the house, I found the two men continuing to alternate in giving mouth-to-mouth resuscitation to the twenty-nine-year-old patient. While the friend took his turn, the husband told me that his wife had been taking medication for severe hypertension for several months, and that just before she collapsed she grabbed the back of her head and complained of a sudden severe headache.

I examined her and found her heart and circulatory system in good shape but the respiratory center in her brain apparently paralyzed. I diagnosed an acute subarachnoid hemorrhage. (This is a sudden massive bleeding at the base of the brain due to a ruptured artery. Such hemorrhages are often caused by an aneurysm, or weak spot in the artery which balloons out and sometimes bursts open.) I told the husband that we had to get his wife to the hospital as quickly as possible. He wasn't sure: Was I positive of the diagnosis? he asked.

I got on the telephone and called Dr. A. C. Silverman, then chief of the Communicable Disease Hospital in Syracuse and an expert in the treatment of poliomyelitis. At this time, iron lungs were still being used to "breathe" for patients paralyzed by polio. I told him our problem, and he suggested that we put my patient in an iron lung. He also asked me if I had a spinal needle with me. When I said yes, he asked me to do a lumbar puncture and call him back with the findings. I did so, and found bright red gross blood, indicating severe bleeding within the spinal cord, with this blood mixing with cerebrospinal fluid. I called Dr. Silverman back, and he said, "If you can get her here we'll put her in a respirator."

Meanwhile, the two men were still performing continuous mouth-to-mouth resuscitation on her. I checked her again, finding her heart condition stable and her pulse and color good. I called an ambulance and the New York State Troopers. By this time it was about 8:30. Within a short time, a snowplow, an ambulance, and two state troopers in their vehicles were lined up in front of the house, ready to take the woman about forty miles to Syracuse.

With the two men still keeping up mouth-to-mouth resuscitation, we got the woman into the ambulance. The snowplow led the way through the fierce snowstorm, followed by one state trooper, followed by the ambulance, followed by the second state trooper. Even with all the help, it took two and a half hours to get the patient to the ambulance entrance of the hospital.

When the cavalcade set off, I remained behind, calling a close friend and colleague of mine, Dr. Jerome Alderman, who practiced neuro-psychiatry in Syracuse. I asked him to attend to my patient at the hospital. Agreeing, he met the entourage when it arrived at the Communicable Disease Hospital in Syracuse. The woman was immediately placed in an iron lung, and Dr. Alderman did all he could. Unfortunately, all the efforts were to no avail; the woman died the following afternoon.

Dr. Alderman called me to tell me the sad news. He also told me how impressed he was by the dedication of the woman's husband and friend who had continued to give her mouth-to-mouth resuscitation throughout the long drive to the hospital. "You should have seen them when they arrived, Marv," he told me. "I've never seen such a sight. Their mouths and faces were covered with frothy sputum, and their lips were swollen to the point of distortion. What a feat!"

In fact, the two men had kept the woman alive with their breath for eight and a half hours—one of the longest periods of time ever documented for mouth-to-mouth resuscitation.

This case occurred in the early fifties. Although this woman died, there was at least an ambulance available to get her to the hospital. When I began my practice, no ambulance service existed on the North Shore. Instead, I had the responsibility of transporting patients to the hospital myself.

I used a system invented by my predecessor, Dr. Melamed. In effect, I transformed my car into a homemade ambulance. I would always drive a two-door car for this reason. Whenever I bought a new car, I would take it down to Harold Morse's garage. He would remove the partition between the back seat of the car and the trunk, increasing the usable length of the passenger compartment. I would always carry in the trunk a large board about the size of a single bed, hinged in the middle for storage, and a mattress to cover it when it was used.

When a patient needed transportation to a hospital, I would remove the back of the back seat, fold down the passenger seat next to me, open out the hinged board, and place the mattress on it. I would put the patient on the mattress, lying on his back with his head resting on top of the folded down passenger seat beside me; this way, I could check him frequently as I drove. Usually I borrowed sheets and blankets from the patient's family, returning them as soon as possible.

I drove patients to hospitals in Oneida and Syracuse in this improvised ambulance countless times. At first, some of the hospital personnel regarded my appearances as rather a joke. Soon, however, they got used to my turning up at the ambulance entrances and were there to greet me, often congratulating me on the way I handled my patients.

About 1945, however, a relative newcomer arrived in the Cleveland area. James Avery was the maintenance manager of the Rome State School's garage. When he moved from Rome to Cleveland, he decided that something better than my homemade ambulance should be available for people on the North Shore. Also, he didn't like the fact that these trips took

HOUSE CALLS

me away from the office for hours at a time. So he began a one-man crusade to raise the funds to buy an ambulance and support its service. Gradually, other people joined his cause: Harold Morse, Arthur Lawson, Kenneth Godfrey, and Robert Landgraff had joined him in his efforts by 1948. They solicited money from local citizens and also from the many vacationers who flooded the North Shore every summer.

By the end of the summer of 1949, Jim Avery had raised enough money to buy his "ambulance." It was a second-hand hearse that he bought from Tom Cox, an undertaker in Rome, who also served as an Oneida County coroner for many years. Richard Tyler, who presently runs a garage in Cleveland, repainted the hearse as an ambulance and installed flashing lights. Once it was ready, it was housed in the Cleveland Volunteer Fire Hall.

Jim's wife, Florence Avery, acted as secretary/treasurer for the operation; their home phone number became the official number to call for ambulance service. Florence was available most of the time; when she wasn't, members of her family generally took her place. The Averys' telephone is still the ambulance phone number on the North Shore. There were no fees for this service; whatever a patient wanted to pay went into a common fund.

The new service was a great boon to me. Whenever I needed to transfer a patient to a hospital, I would call up Florence, who would call one of the volunteer drivers: Harold Morse, Kenneth Godfrey, or Arthur Lawson. When the ambulance arrived, I would help load up the patient, and if medical attention was necessary I would ride along in the ambulance.

In two years, Tom Cox's hearse had outlived its usefulness, and a second hearse was bought to replace it. Two years later, the community was able to afford a Cadillac hearse. Finally, in 1957, we were able to buy a real secondhand ambulance from the Catskill, New York, rescue squad. By 1962 the Cleveland Volunteer Fire Department had taken over management of the ambulance service and had set up crews that were available for ambulance duty around the clock.

All this time, Florence Avery acted as the dispatcher, and her husband Jim remained one of the volunteer drivers. Even after he had a heart attack in 1961, Jim refused to give up this work. Only his death in 1965 ended his involvement.

In the early seventies the ambulance crews were taught first aid, and later C.P.R. In the late seventies they were given courses in life support and advanced life support. By this time two modern ambulances were in service, and the crews would answer calls around the clock. They could now perform I.V.s, use a defibrillator, take E.K.G.s, and perform emergency treatment under the direction of a doctor received by two-way radio from hospitals in Oneida, Rome, and Syracuse.

These days I would give the North Shore Ambulance Service a top rating for its service to the citizens of the area. When a call comes in, the ambulance responds within five to ten minutes, depending on the distance it must travel to pick up a patient.

Since 1980, the ambulance service has been hooked into a countywide ambulance system with a single dispatcher in the city of Oswego; finally the Avery household has been relieved of its constant surveillance, and the job of treasurer has been passed to a new generation of Averys. But when I recall the beginnings of the service, I realize how great a debt the North Shore owes the Avery family.

The history of the ambulance service in Cleveland points to another aspect of my rural practice that helped still my doubts and keep me going: the tremendous cooperation I received from my patients, their families, and, indeed, all the local people. With aid from other medical professionals unavailable most of the time in my early years of practice, I relied for help on the people who were around, and for the most part they came through heroically.

As my practice (and income) grew, however, I was finally able to afford some paid help around our home and office. If

HOUSE CALLS

Bee and I were ever to escape from our busy lives, someone had to be at home to care for our children and answer telephone calls for me. Goldie Stinger became our first regular helper, and Molly Godfrey filled in when needed. Both ladies were very competent and reliable. Their presence allowed me to take Thursdays away from the office.

Usually on Thursdays, therefore, Bee and I would head for Syracuse for the day. I would visit any of my patients who were hospitalized, we would both visit relatives and friends, and then we usually had dinner together in a restaurant before coming home. Those dinners were important to us—an hour or two snatched out of the week when we could be alone together again.

Even with a stand-in at home, however, these Thursdays away often posed problems. What if messages had come in during my absence that I was needed for house calls? In time I arranged a system of signals that would alert me that I was needed and save some traveling time. It worked like this: If patients called my office on Thursdays needing attention, whoever was helping at our home would direct my patients to call Mrs. Hazel Farnett. She operated a grocery store in the village of Constantia that we passed on our way home. If I was needed, she would put a light on in her store window. I would stop, get the messages, and go on to make the necessary calls.

I had a similar arrangement for days when I went to Oneida or Utica. If we were returning from that direction, Mrs. Irene Montross, whose husband ran a garage in North Bay, would put a light on in her living room to signal that I was needed in the area. For years, these women responded to their neighbors' calls or hand-delivered messages to "put the light on." I will never forget their help; it saved me countless hours of traveling time. The only drawback to this signal system was that when I did have calls to make, Bee was a captive and had to go along with me.

In 1941, I hired my first professional helper, Mrs. Frances Hooper. Mrs. Hooper's parents had recently moved into a house

A HARD DAY'S NIGHT

nearby. Her mother, in her mid-seventies, had severe, crippling rheumatoid arthritis; her spine and joints were frozen almost completely. Her father was a retired tool and die maker also in his mid-seventies. Papa Neal, as we called him, had devised many clever homemade aids for his wife, including a lift and hammock apparatus to help her get into the bath or bed, or onto the toilet. But he still needed help in managing, so he asked his daughter to come and live with them in Cleveland.

Mrs. Hooper therefore wrote to me, asking for a job. She wanted at least $50 a month, which would keep her afloat financially. She had good qualifications. In her mid-forties, she was a licensed practical nurse, a licensed masseuse, and could also type and keep books. I was a little doubtful that I could afford to pay her what she was asking, but I decided to take a chance. It was a very smart move; Hoopey, as we called her, turned out to be a gem—a real friend in need.

Since I had only a two-room office, one room of which was the waiting room, I hired her to work for three hours in the morning while I was out making house calls or working at the hospital. If she had been there all the time we would have been constantly in each other's way. Hoopey was a whirlwind of activity from the beginning; answering the telephone, doing the books, typing my letters, handling the patients with skill and warmth, and even taking care of our children on Thursdays or most any time we were out. She soon became an honorary member of our family, and in time her father too was drawn into the circle.

Since they lived across the street from us, she was right there for emergencies. I taught her how to help me on home deliveries, and the two of us traveled about the countryside at all hours, bringing babies into the world.

Even in later years, after she left Cleveland, she was only a telephone call away when we needed her to take over during our absences. In all the years we have known her, she has never let us down.

HOUSE CALLS

Hoopey was the first of several nurses and secretaries whom I trained to help me on emergency house calls—especially home deliveries. Once such professional—or at least trained—assistance was available to me, the responsibilities of my practice did not seem so huge, and the rewards seemed to multiply.

Four
Placebos and Mudholes

"You'll be working under less-than-ideal conditions a lot of the time without good backup. But you'll never be bored." So Dr. Melamed had told me when I first came to Cleveland to look over his practice. As I settled into life in Cleveland, I found both statements to be perfectly true.

For one thing, country life seems to give people a lot of scope to develop eccentricities. For another, the rural brand of poverty, especially in the early years of my practice, meant that I often had to work in very primitive conditions, and to deal with the disturbing effects of ignorance arising out of this poverty. Moreover, the problems of a rural practice also included dealing with the different sort of ignorance displayed by city vacationers and hunters visiting the area. All of these things made my work at times taxing, irritating, tragic, even frightening—but never dull.

One of the first eccentrics I encountered in Cleveland was Marion Morenus. A petite, wizened woman with sharp features and bright eyes, Marion was a very successful antique dealer. She knew the antique trade thoroughly, and her business acumen was remarkable. She lived alone on Bridge Street in a small two-story house stuffed with lovely antiques.

At the time I arrived in Cleveland, Marion had already gained a reputation as an eccentric. Although she came from an old, established family, she was a loner who shunned most of the social events of the area. This may have been due partly to embarrassment over her ill-fitting dentures; they clicked, making it hard to understand her. Embarrassment didn't hold Marion back in business, however. No one ever got the better of her in a business deal; she always had a ready answer when driving a bargain.

Marion was also a hypochondriac—and always expected instant attention from her doctor. She would call me at all hours, mostly for insignificant complaints, and insist that I come right over. It made no difference to her if it was 3:00 P.M. or 3:00 A.M.—and she didn't see that it should make a difference to me. She would lie in state in her beautiful curly maple bed with its hand-hewn posts and wait for me to attend her. She refused to visit my office; I had to go to her. In all the years I treated her, she never came to me.

The first time I visited her, she showed me her medicine cabinet, filled with bottles of pills. When I asked her what they were, she had no idea; instead she referred to them by color. "The red ones are my headache pills," she told me. "The green ones are for nausea. I take the yellow ones when my palpitations come on, and the purple ones are for depression." On she went, listing her stockpile by color, and she seemed impatient when I told her the names and functions of the medications I prescribed for her. I was disturbed by her cache of pills, and this unease grew when our common cleaning woman, Goldie Stinger, told Bee that every morning Marion would choose the pills she would take that day by color.

I soon found out the truth of the matter, however. Apparently my predecessor, Dr. Melamed, had sized up Marion's true medical needs quite early on. He had given her a range of placebos differentiated by color and had told her she could take them as she needed them. It was a system that gave Marion what she most needed—reassurance—without side effects. I soon adopted it, and before long she and I were getting along famously.

PLACEBOS AND MUDHOLES

As the years passed, Marion developed the usual vascular diseases of aging, and I had to treat her with real medicines instead of the colored pills she favored. In her late seventies, she broke first one hip and then, two years later, the other. When she was in the hospital getting the second hip pinned, Bee visited her. She was doing well, but this didn't seem to cheer her. "Please, Bee," she said, "pray for me to die. I'm running out of money, and I don't want to go on relief." In fact, however, she recovered well and was able to return home. And although she lived to be ninety-three years old, she never did need public assistance.

Another woman famous in the Cleveland area for her eccentricities was Rosamond Gifford. She was a very wealthy recluse who lived in a large home, part of a large estate, about half a mile east of Cleveland. Rosamond had inherited her money from her father, who had owned a huge tract of land just east of Syracuse. When I was a young boy, the beginning of the Gifford tract marked the limits of the city of Syracuse on the east side. During the twenties, the Gifford tract was divided into hundreds of building lots, and the entire area was later incorporated into Syracuse.

The money from the land passed to Rosamond, but despite her wealth she chose to live alone with the help of only a single hired man, Charles Schmidt. He came down daily from his home on Kathryn Street in Cleveland to attend to her needs. One of his main chores was the milking of her herd of forty goats. In cold weather, they were housed in a barn near the house— a solid structure with a hardwood floor formerly used for horses. In good weather, they were put out to graze on the lakeshore lot of the estate. Their milk was used to feed an army of cats that roamed freely in the house.

During our early days in Cleveland, Bee's various charitable drives often led her to approach Rosamond for donations. But without fail, whether Bee asked in person or by phone, Rosamond directed Charles to turn her away.

51

HOUSE CALLS

I was called only once to treat Rosamond. Charles called and told me that she had fallen and landed on her left shoulder, dislocating it. "She wants you to come and put it back, Doc," said Charles. "She told me to tell you to come to the barn."

I drove through the gloomy fall evening to the Gifford place and picked my way to the barn. Rosamond stood in the dim light inside holding her left shoulder with her right hand: A chunky woman of sixty, her disheveled gray hair was pulled back with a rubber band, her frame swallowed in a dirty, dark woolen skirt and gray shawl sweater, her feet shod in the felt boots commonly worn by farmers in the area.

I examined her shoulder gently. "You've dislocated it all right," I said. "Let's go in the house, and I'll reduce it for you."

"Oh, no, doctor," she answered. "This happens fairly often and usually I can put it back myself. I couldn't this time, but there's no need to go to the house. I'll lay on some of these bales of hay." As she spoke she kicked two bales together, and Charles and I helped her onto them. She lay on her back, and it took only a simple twist to replace the shoulder joint. Rosamond jumped off the improvised bed, much relieved. She swung her left arm back and forth and said, "That feels fine now. How much do I owe you?"

"Five dollars," I said. Rosamond reached down into her bosom and pulled out a leather drawstring wallet stuffed with bills. She separated a five dollar bill from the wad and handed it to me.

"Thank you, doctor," she said, and turned away. Charles let me out, and I drove home.

Many years later when she died, Rosamond left a charitable trust fund of several million dollars, now administered by a board of leading Syracuse citizens. Her name is justly honored in the Syracuse area. For me, however, her name will always evoke a solitary figure dressed in farmer's clothes, hugging her shoulder, in the dim light of the barn.

Many people believe that wealth excuses—or at least

PLACEBOS AND MUDHOLES

explains—oddity or imperiousness of manner. This argument may apply to Rosamond Gifford and Marion Morenus, but it doesn't apply to Jacob Fidler. Yet his expectations of attention from me were at least as insistent as Marion's.

The Fidlers lived about nine miles north of Constantia village, a short distance off the main road in a place called the Holly Hole. "Hole" was a good name for it. Each spring after the winter snows had melted, the road there literally fell in. It became a sea of gooey mud. Several times on house calls there in the spring I had to get help to prevent my car from being swallowed up completely.

The Fidlers' house resembled a movie set for the Kentucky hillbillies. And their way of life wasn't far off either. Jacob was the head of the family. He was a very gaunt man around seventy years old—a good deal older than his wife. Often when I arrived, he was settled in a rocking chair on the porch, wearing blue overalls, and smoking a corncob pipe. He was a crochety old man, and like Marion Morenus, expected me to come immediately when he called. Since he had no way of getting into Cleveland to my office, I had no choice but to go to him.

One Sunday in July, at 4:30 in the morning, Jacob called me, seeming quite upset.

"Doc, you gotta come up. Something awful happened to me!" he said.

"What seems to be the trouble?" I asked.

"I can't tell you. It's something on my hand. It's awful. You gotta come up."

I sighed. "Could you come down?" I asked. "Maybe a neighbor would drive you in?"

"I have no way of getting down," was his answer. "You gotta come up, Doc, now!"

It was just dawn as I set out. The sun was coming up gloriously, promising a beautiful day. The air was fresh and still cool from the night. I regretted being out of my warm bed but felt a little compensated by the lovely sunrise. Since it was July,

53

HOUSE CALLS

I managed to get my car through the mudhole near the Fidlers' with little trouble. When I reached their house, Jacob was sitting in his rocker in the kitchen, holding onto his right thumb.

"What's the matter, Jake?" I asked.

He pointed to the base of his right thumb. "There. That's it."

I looked closely, but I couldn't see anything abnormal except a small scratch. "Is this it?" I asked.

"Yes," Jacob said. "Something scratched or bit me there last night, and I couldn't sleep at all, thinking about it. Do you suppose a deadly spider got me?"

I looked again at the tiny scratch and swallowed hard. "I . . . think it'll be all right, Jacob. I'm sure it's nothing to worry about. But just to make sure I'll wash it and put some iodine on it. O.K.?"

I carefully washed his thumb and swabbed a little iodine on it. "There," I said. "Everything will be fine now."

"Thanks, Doc," said Jacob. "Thanks for coming up." I took my leave, got into my car, and drove away. Once away from Holly Hole, I laughed until my stomach hurt. I had gotten up at 4:30 in the morning and driven a thirty-mile round trip to attend to a scratch on a thumb. Certainly what doctors regard as emergencies and what patients regard as emergencies can be as different as apples and oranges! At least I got a beautiful sunrise out of it.

Not too long after this, however, Jacob called me back to Holly Hole for an emergency rather more serious than a scratched thumb. "Doc Brown? My daughter fell and hurt her right arm. It's really crooked, and it sure looks busted," he said. "Can you come up right away?"

This time it was a reasonable hour of the day, and the emergency seemed genuine. I collected Hoopey, took my open mask, a can of ether, some dressings and plaster of paris, and set out on the fifteen-mile drive.

Sure enough, Jacob's seven-year-old daughter had greenstick

PLACEBOS AND MUDHOLES

fractures of the mid-radius and ulna of her right forearm. (Both bones in her forearm were broken, but not completely through.) The breaks were so obvious that I didn't need an X-ray for this diagnosis. We put the girl on the Fidlers' kitchen table. Hoopey poured the ether to put her to sleep. Then I straightened out the fractures and applied a cast with the plaster of paris. In time, the bones healed straight and solid.

This incident illustrates the rough and ready conditions under which I often had to work. With many patients unable to make the trip into the village, I had to do the best I could in the prevailing conditions. Setting Jacob's daughter's arm was easy compared with some of the jobs that confronted me over the years.

One occasion that tried my ingenuity to the utmost took place in early 1941 when I was called to the home of the Mooney family to attend a birth. The Mooneys lived on a dirt road near Constantia Center. Robert, the father, was a hard-working man who managed to keep his large family fed and clothed despite the hard times the Depression brought. His wife developed rheumatic heart disease but seemed to weather her many pregnancies well in spite of it. By the time she was in her forties she needed supportive treatment and seemed to be in partial heart failure most of the time. I staved off a complete heart failure by giving her intravenous injections of mercurial diuretics twice a week.

One day, Mrs. Mooney brought her thirteen-year-old daughter to my office for examination. I soon found that the girl was well advanced into pregnancy. The prospective father was a nice hard-working man of about twenty years of age, who wanted nothing more than to marry the Mooney girl. He intended to prepare a home for her with new furniture and all the necessities. These plans had been made with the Mooneys' full blessing; however, it had been decided that the wedding should wait until after the baby was born.

One evening in March, I got the message that the Mooney

HOUSE CALLS

girl had gone into labor and I was needed at their house. The birth that followed was one of the most unusual home deliveries I ever took part in. The girl had had her fourteenth birthday a month earlier, and she had matured physically to such a degree during her pregnancy that I had expected no trouble with the delivery. Indeed, there was none; it was the conditions in which I delivered the baby that were unusual.

The Mooneys had no electricity in their house, and the girl's labor continued well past sundown. She labored in a small loft bedroom, lying across a bed that just about fit in the room. The edge of the bed came to the top of the steep stairway which provided access to the room. This stairway was almost as steep as a ladder; and, since there was no room to stand in the loft, I had to stand on its steps with only my upper body rising into the loft. Mrs. Mooney managed to get onto the bed with her daughter so that she could hold cold cloths to the girl's forehead and console her during the labor pains. Since it was very dark, Mr. Mooney stood below me on the stair, shining the six-celled flashlight I always carried with me over my shoulder so that I could see what I was doing. Flickering light from a kerosene lantern in the kitchen below added a surreal cast to the whole scene.

Despite the primitive conditions, the Mooney girl delivered a fine baby girl spontaneously, and the whole family seemed to rejoice.

About two weeks later, the proud parents applied for a marriage license. However, the town clerk, realizing the youth of the girl, refused to issue it. Instead, she notified the children's section of the County Social Service Department. Since, legally, the twenty-year-old was guilty of first degree rape (intercourse with a minor being so defined), the couple was forced to appear before the county judge. The families of both young people appeared at the court hearing, however, and explained that they were in favor of the marriage. Under the circumstances, the judge decided to dismiss the rape charge. He said the marriage could take place in two years, when the bride-to-be would reach the age of sixteen.

Accordingly, two years later, the young couple appeared in my office with their two-year-old, asking if I would take their blood tests so that they could be married. I did so with pleasure, and at last they set up housekeeping together—in a new house with new furniture, just as the new husband had promised.

Another unusual maternity case that I will never forget was the delivery of Mrs. Burton Wright's first baby one bitter cold morning in February 1961. The Wrights had called early the previous evening to tell me that Mrs. Wright was in active labor, so I had set off at once for the Wrights' small home. My secretary Peg (Margaret Oatman), whom I had trained to assist at home deliveries, came with me.

The Wrights were a young married couple. They had little money, but they were honest and hardworking, and one had to admire their courage. They had built their home themselves—a tiny log cabin about twenty miles from Cleveland, north of Williamstown. The cabin consisted of a kitchen, bedroom, and living room, with an outhouse providing the toilet facilities. The cabin's only sources of heat were a wood-burning stove in the kitchen and a fireplace in the living room.

It was a clear night and bitter cold, with the temperature below zero. When Peg and I arrived at the Wrights', there was a roaring fire in the fireplace, but even so we were cold. Except for the actual delivery, we both kept our coats on all the time we were there.

We arrived about 10:30 P.M., and the baby wasn't born until about 3:30 the following morning. I used sterile rubber gloves to examine Mrs. Wright several times during the labor. I couldn't use ether because of the open fire, but Mrs. Wright was a brave young woman and worked hard with her contractions. When the delivery was near, Peg and I placed Mrs. Wright across the width of her bed and went to work. We were warm on the side facing the fireplace, but our backsides were cold!

HOUSE CALLS

I used a local anesthetic for the episiotomy; the baby came down and was delivered spontaneously, the afterbirth followed, and, with Peg massaging Mrs. Wright's lower abdomen, I repaired the episiotomy as well as I could. I must have done a good job, because in her later deliveries the repair appeared to hold up very well.

I had many patients in my practice like the Fidlers, Mooneys, and Wrights, who were very poor but also responsible, hardworking community members and caring toward their families. Sadly, I also encountered a few families whose poverty was compounded by ignorance and neglect.

The Roberts family is a case in point. Even before I took over the practice, Dr. Melamed warned me about them in no uncertain terms. The Roberts lived in Constantia Center, not far from the Mooneys, in an old wooden house near the village cemetery. The family consisted of Joe Roberts, his wife, and several children. I was told that they lived in squalor. They had no toilet—not even an outhouse—and simply went outdoors to relieve themselves. Joe earned some money by trapping and hunting in the woods nearby. Deer and game were always plentiful, and a garden supplied them with vegetables. Joe also earned money by acting as caretaker for several summer properties in the area, and this enabled him to buy staples such as sugar, salt, flour, and a minimum of clothing. An old potbelly stove, fueled with wood, heated the home and acted as the cookstove on which water was heated and food prepared; the water came from a nearby stream as there was no indoor plumbing.

Shortly before I arrived in Cleveland, Dr. Melamed had a run-in with Joe Roberts that alarmed him considerably. Mrs. Roberts became pregnant regularly and the family grew rapidly. A doctor was called in to deliver their first child, but thereafter Joe Roberts delivered his children himself. He would express the afterbirth and then tie the umbilical cord with a piece of twine that he would bite off in his mouth. Only after this would he call Dr. Melamed to come up to his house and fill out a

PLACEBOS AND MUDHOLES

birth certificate.

Luck seemed to be on his side for some time. The babies survived and thrived. However, one delivery did not end so smoothly. On this occasion, the baby was born without trouble and Joe tied the cord in his usual way. On the third day after the birth, he called in Dr. Melamed to issue a birth certificate. When Dr. Melamed arrived, however, he was frightened by the appearance of the baby. The abdominal area around the tied cord was markedly red and swollen, and purulent matter was oozing from the stump of the umbilicus. Clearly, a serious infection had set in. Since this was early in 1938, before antibiotics were widely available, Dr. Melamed told the Roberts' to apply continuous warm, wet compresses and to try to get extra water into the baby, in addition to breast-feeding it.

Dr. Melamed returned the next day to check up on the baby, but as he approached the house he was stopped by Joe Roberts, who stood on a rise nearby and threatened Dr. Melamed with a shotgun.

"Don't come any closer, or I'll shoot," Joe shouted. "You killed my baby!" The baby had apparently died from the infection contracted from the dirty tied cord. But since its condition had worsened after Dr. Melamed's first visit, Joe Roberts blamed Dr. Melamed for its death. Dr. Melamed left as quickly as possible and notified the county authorities of the baby's death. The county investigated but found that the baby had died of natural causes in its own home. No charges were filed against Roberts, but Dr. Melamed gave me a strong warning about the family.

Almost three years later, on November 6, 1940, I was called by Joe Roberts to come up to the house to sign a death certificate for one of his children. He said only that the baby, then six months old, had suddenly died. Since the child's death was unattended by a doctor and seemed suspicious, I called the district attorney's office and reported the circumstances. He ordered the local undertaker to take the baby's body to me for an autopsy.

I had not done an autopsy since I was on staff at the St.

59

HOUSE CALLS

Lawrence State Hospital, but I suspected that the baby might have died of fulminating pneumonia, so, wanting to make sure, I accepted the challenge. In my capacity as coroner's physician I did a partial autopsy and found the baby's lungs to be solid with inflammation. I reported that death had indeed been caused by pneumonia, and since this was a natural cause of death the body was released for burial and no charges were filed. Even so, I often think of that little baby and wonder how much the poverty and ignorance of its parents contributed to its condition and eventual death.

In the case of another child I treated many years later, there was no doubt that her parent's ignorance was the direct cause of her condition. In this instance, the mother brought the child, a four-year-old girl, into my office for treatment. She said the girl wasn't growing.

When I asked what she meant, the mother took off her daughter's clothes and exposed her body. What I saw then stunned and frightened me. All the girl's limbs were shortened and deformed. There seemed to be thickening under the skin and evidence that the limbs had been broken fairly recently.

"What happened to her?" I asked, trying to stay calm.

For an answer, the mother grasped one of the girl's forearms in her two hands and began to snap it as one would snap a piece of wood in two. I reached out quickly and stopped her from proceeding any further. Then she said, "I came to you to find out why my girl's arms and legs are not growing right. She cries a lot too, especially when I try to help her grow by snapping her arms and legs."

I immediately reported the case to the children's section of the Oswego County Department of Social Services. After investigation, the child was placed in a foster home, and the mother was diagnosed as retarded and placed under supervision. My heart still fills with pity for the child, though, who had suffered damage that could never be undone.

Rural ignorance was not the only kind I had to cope with,

however. There were other occasions when the ignorance of city folks visiting the area proved equally disastrous. I remember clearly one such occasion in 1970. It was one Sunday morning about 11:00 during the hunting season. I was on the patio of our home reading the Sunday paper when two men in hunting clothes came running up.

"Are you the doctor?"

"Yes," I replied.

"Then come with us. We've had a terrible hunting accident."

I followed them around to the driveway in front of my office, and there on a makeshift stretcher—an old door they'd found in the woods—lay a young man, apparently in shock. He had been shot accidentally in the abdomen. His two companions had had to carry him about two miles through the woods. Then they placed him on the floor of their van and drove into Cleveland. By the time they found me, his clothes were saturated with blood, and the entrance wound in his abdomen was oozing yet more blood. His color was very poor, and his pulse rapid and weak.

I rushed into the office, returning quickly with a dose of morphine. Then I placed a tight compress dressing on the wound. Next I called Dr. Leon Berman at the old University Hospital of the Good Shepherd in Syracuse. I told him what had happened and asked him to get things ready for the arrival of my patient. When the wounded man arrived at the hospital, the operating room was all ready for him. There Dr. Berman, with his associates, worked long and hard to save him. Several blood transfusions later, the careful and difficult surgery was over. The team had repaired the man's bowel where possible, and taken out parts too damaged to repair. Fortunately, the bullet had missed the patient's liver and other vital organs. Their efforts paid off; the man survived.

By chance I met this patient again many years later. Bee and I were leaving the Syracuse Civic Center after a concert one evening when I overheard this conversation between two men directly behind us:

"How are things going, Harold?"

"Well, pretty good now. It took awhile, though, for me to recover from that gunshot wound. Did you know about that? Doc Berman put me back together again after a country doctor in Cleveland gave me emergency treatment."

Hearing this, I casually looked over my shoulder. Then the questioner tapped me on the shoulder and said, "Marv! Harold, this is your country doctor!" Harold Miller and I were introduced by our mutual friend, and he and his wife both thanked me for saving his life. It was a gratifying end to a good evening.

I was often honored by the aid and friendship given me by my patients. This was the obverse side of the coin of rural practice; I had to contend with many problems of communication and distance, poverty and ignorance, but I was also able to draw on the strong sense of community found in rural areas and was often pleased beyond measure by signs of appreciation from my patients.

One patient of mine who gave me both aid and appreciation was Fred Collier. Fred ran a feed and coal business in Cleveland for many years, operating out of an old wooden feed mill located on Center Street. For many years, that mill solved a problem for me. My office weight scale recorded weights only up to 250 pounds. Unfortunately, I had a number of patients who weighed more than that. I was at a loss to get an accurate measure of their weights until Fred allowed me to use his feed scale for the purpose. I used his scale in this way for many years, until, five years after Fred's death, a fire consumed the building. After that, I had to estimate the weights of my obese patients for my records.

Fred had lung cancer. He bore it bravely until June 1947, when he died at the age of sixty-eight. One of his dying requests surprised and touched me. He asked that I play my violin at his funeral. I had always bragged a bit about my violin playing, and since coming to Cleveland I had played a few times at square dances at the village fire hall and later at the new school. I wasn't really that good, but I guess my playing pleased Fred. So at his request and his family's insistence I played at his funeral on that beautiful warm day. A microphone was set up on the lawn in front of the Collier house on Clay Street. Galene Doque, a candy maker in Cleveland, sang in her beautiful contralto voice, and I accompanied her. It was a moving occasion for me; I felt like part of a community in a way that is rare today. Oddly enough, though, I have never received any more requests to play at funerals!

Five
A Little Help from My Colleagues

The sense of community I found when I was living and working in Cleveland was one of the greatest rewards of the life I had chosen. But in addition to this rural community that enclosed both Bee and me, I soon found myself a part of another, separate community: a community of professionals.

Once I felt I had settled into my work in Cleveland, I began to think about reestablishing links with the wider medical world. Accordingly, I decided to join the local county medical society. Since I lived in Oswego County, I first decided to join its society. This group met once a month on Tuesday nights in the cities of either Oswego or Fulton. I began attending these meetings regularly and soon became a member. At the same time, I joined the New York State Medical Society and the American Medical Association.

After going to several of the Oswego County Medical Society meetings, however, I began to realize that there was a rift between the doctors from Fulton and those from Oswego. This was discouraging, as I wanted to be involved in a cooperative, friendly group. Even more discouraging was the forty-two-mile drive to Oswego over narrow twisting roads, often in bad weather.

HOUSE CALLS

Furthermore, I had recently begun using the Oneida City Hospital, in Madison County, as my hospital of record. All of these factors led me, after only a short time, to change my allegiance from the Oswego County Medical Society to that of Madison County. I wrote to the New York State Medical Society for permission to do so and was soon granted it by the council of the state society.

Membership in the Madison County Medical Society put me in touch with other doctors who had interests and problems similar to my own. We had many lively discussions on everything from local medical problems to matters of medical politics and national trends. I remained an active member for the rest of my medical career, becoming its president for the year of 1954-55. Recently I became a life member, a status allowing me to vote but not serve as an officer.

I found the county society illuminating and stimulating. However, it was my association with the Oneida City Hospital that really gave me the sense of medical comradeship I had been looking for. This was a great relief, for, even in the short time I had been practicing, I had been disquieted by some of the medical practices I had already witnessed. I recall, particularly, my first experience with a physician who was a staff member at the Rome City Hospital.

I had been called to attend a young woman who had recently moved to Cleveland from Rome, New York. I diagnosed her as having an acute appendicitis, and I suggested that she go immediately into the hospital for surgery. However, since I was still young and had been in practice a fairly short time, her family hesitated and said they wished first to consult with their own doctor in Rome. He came to Cleveland and examined her, and, confirming my diagnosis, soon arranged for her to be taken to the Rome City Hospital.

As we waited for the ambulance to take her there, I asked this doctor who would do the surgery.

"I will," he answered. "I work with two other physicians,

and we rotate on surgical cases. For each operation one is in charge, one assists, and the third gives the anesthesia, with the responsibilities changing each time. This time it's my turn to perform the surgery."

I was shocked at this picture of three generalists casually rotating jobs in surgery, regardless of their skill. I soon found, however, that some generalists practiced this way routinely, doing everything allowable from taking care of colds to performing abdominal surgery to giving general anesthesia. In this case, all went well, and the young woman made an uneventful recovery. But I was still determined to find a medical community that provided fruitful, skilled cooperation.

When I first began taking patients to the Oneida City Hospital, I was also discouraged once again. At that time, it was virtually run by Dr. Eugene Carpenter, Sr., who was then in his eighties. Dr. Carpenter had begun practicing medicine in a more rough and ready age, and his methods had not changed. I remember once in those early days arriving with a patient in my homemade ambulance. Dr. Carpenter met me and asked for my diagnosis.

"Acute appendicitis," I answered.

"All right," he said, and turning to a nurse, ordered, "Prepare him for immediate surgery."

I was staggered. "Aren't you going to examine him or make any tests? Confirm my diagnosis?" I asked.

"Your diagnosis is good enough for me," he answered.

Still rather surprised, I followed him up to the scrub room. There he introduced me to his son, Eugene, Jr., who had only recently finished a surgical residency.

"Do you want to assist my father or give the anesthesia?" Eugene asked me. "I don't mind which I do."

Once again I was shocked. As at Rome, it seemed that the job you performed in surgery didn't depend on your skill or area of expertise. I opted to assist. Luckily my diagnosis proved to be correct; my patient did have an acute appendicitis, and

HOUSE CALLS

the operation did in fact turn out to have been necessary.

To my relief, it wasn't long before this casual brand of medical practice was abandoned at the Oneida City Hospital. Most of the physicians who practiced there during my years of practice were of the highest caliber. And most of them were G.P.s with a few specialists among them, but all helped one another when necessary.

As I look back, the cooperation that existed there was very much like group practice found today, but in a hospital setting. The surgical dressing rooms, the patients' rooms, the delivery and surgical rooms and the corridors of the hospital became the learning centers where much of my post-graduate education was garnered. Whenever I needed a consultation, I received it. I would call on any of the doctors there at any time, day or night. They never hesitated to help me out, especially in an emergency.

I often needed such help. I knew what I could handle and what there was no sense in attempting. Knowing the limits of my expertise and getting help when a problem fell outside them has always been my policy as a generalist, and my patients knew this and respected me for it.

Delighted to have found such comrades in medicine, I soon joined the Oneida City Hospital as a member in good standing of its staff. In 1938, to become a hospital staff member, a physician had to prove that he was of good moral standing and character, was in good physical and mental health, could practice medicine, and had the necessary degrees and certificates to prove it. I had no trouble satisfying these conditions, but in the beginning I got quite tired of having to prove this to the nurses. I remember arriving there for the first time with a patient in my homemade ambulance. I was unloading him when the nursing supervisor sailed out and asked me what I was doing there. It took me some time to prove to her satisfaction that I really was old enough to be a fully qualified doctor! I was challenged so often those first few months that I decided I had to make myself look older.

So I went out and bought a pair of horn-rimmed glasses with plain lenses. It was magical! The questions ceased. I continued to wear the glasses in my office and on hospital visits for the first year or two of my practice. The confidence they inspired was well worth the teasing I got from Bee and my friends. It was a tough delivery that finally completed the job of winning the respect of the nursing staff at the Oneida City Hospital, however. After I had delivered one nurse's baby by forceps following a tough and complicated labor, I knew I had passed muster—even with the nursing supervisor.

However, it soon became evident that I could not follow the course nor continue the care of my hospitalized patients except for the normal obstetrical cases. Even without frequent trips to the hospital, I was driving an average of thirty-five thousand miles a year in my practice, making house calls and home deliveries in an area of four hundred square miles. I was putting myself behind the steering wheel of my car when I should have been attending patients who needed me on the North Shore. Frequent trips to the hospital on top of my office work and local calls soon became impossible.

Therefore, I routinely referred my medical cases who needed hospitalization to Dr. Lee Preston, my surgical cases to Dr. Howard Beach, and my pediatric cases to Dr. Ernest Freshman. All three men gave my patients the greatest care possible, and when they were unavailable, other equally competent physicians were usually there to fill in. After their hospitalizations, my patients returned to me for follow-up care. In all the years I followed this arrangement, I don't recall a dissatisfied patient or patient's family, except in rare cases when a doctor unknown to me was on call and admitted my patient.

There were other specialists, too, to whom I referred my patients. My choices were men of high standing and good reputation within the profession; I was determined to obtain the best medical and surgical care I could for my patients.

I tried hard to keep my own hand in at the hospital, despite problems of time and distance. I continued to perform the deliveries of all my normal obstetrical patients there and to assist Dr. Beach at most of my surgical cases, including Caesarean sections. I also gave anesthetics for tonsillectomies, and I filled in at the emergency room at various times. Moreover, when I came to the hospital with a patient, I tried to visit any other patients of mine who were there at the time under the care of my consulting physicians; for these courtesy calls there were no fees.

I kept my involvement at the hospital, however, strictly within the limits of my expertise. The doctors at the Oneida City Hospital made sure that skilled specialists were in charge during operations and that jobs were not rotated indiscriminately.

Over the years I learned a great deal from men like Howard Beach, Lee Preston, and Ernest Freshman. They taught me the art, as well as the science, of medicine, confirming for me the fact that the patient is the prime reason for being in this business of doctoring, all else is secondary.

Two surgical cases at which I assisted, during my years at Oneida, stand out as unusual in my memory. The first was a delivery in which a C-section was needed. Laurence and Esther Cottet were patients of mine in Cleveland. When I came to Cleveland they had been married for several years without having had any children. Then, when Esther was in her mid-thirties, she became pregnant at last. When she went into labor, I took her to the Oneida City Hospital. After some time, however, it became clear that her labor was not progressing satisfactorily. I called in Dr. Beach for a consultation, and he suggested a test of labor for another hour. The hour passed and still there was no progress. Dr. Beach and I decided that a Caesarean section was necessary.

When I assisted at the C-section, the reason for Esther's lack of progress soon became clear. She had a very large benign tumor of the uterus, which was pushing the fetus far to one side. Moreover, the pressure from the tumor had grossly

A LITTLE HELP FROM MY COLLEAGUES

deformed the baby. Once the baby had been delivered, I took over his care while Dr. Beach attended Esther and then assisted in removing her entire uterus. The baby, a boy, had a misshaped head, a deformed ear, and deep dimples in one shoulder, among other problems; however, he survived his traumatic start in life, and as he grew his deformities became much less noticeable. Over my years in Cleveland I watched his progress from a smart little boy to an accomplished citizen of the village. I am grateful for the expertise of Dr. Beach, which helped save his life.

In the second unusual case I recall, I administered the anesthetic when Dr. Crockett, the ophthalmologist and laboratory director at the Oneida City Hospital, performed an eye operation.

The patient was a young boy, one of twins. I had received a frantic call one morning from his mother to come to the house. Her son, eight years old, had been hit in the eye with a stone, and it was bleeding profusely. I dropped everything and drove there immediately. When I examined the boy, the situation looked serious. A small stone had hit his right eye, collapsing the eyeball. I placed a compress bandage over the eye. Then I called my office, and told Bee to call the hospital to alert Dr. Crockett about the case. Quickly, I settled the boy in my ambulance and drove as fast as I could to Oneida. Dr. Crockett was waiting for me in the hospital emergency room. He examined the eye and told me the bad news; the eye would have to come out.

We took the boy to the operating room, and I administered the anesthetic while Dr. Crockett enuncleated the eye. It was a sad occasion; to lose an eye at the age of eight is a bitter blow. Nevertheless, I remember with gratitude Dr. Crockett's prompt help and skilled work.

Dr. Crockett was a character at the Oneida City Hospital. He was tremendously skilled and very dedicated. However, his operating style was, to say the least, unusual. He practically always smoked cigars and would operate without using surgical gloves. I would watch with amazement while he performed cataract operations and other eye surgery using local anesthetics. His

71

instruments were perfectly sterile, and only they would touch the patient. But as he snipped delicately at the eye, he would continue to puff smoke from one of his ever-present cigars. As the nurse sponged the area, he would put his cigar down and flick off the ashes. Then it would go back in his mouth as he began to work upon the eye again. He would cut and suture the eye with the greatest possible care, and tie knots with his small forceps, puffing smoke the whole time. Despite his unorthodox methods, his results were beautiful.

Not all the specialists to whom I referred patients worked at the Oneida City Hospital. In the early days of my practice I would take children who needed tonsillectomies to Dr. Norman Livshin in Syracuse for their operations. Sometimes there would be two patients, sometimes six. The parents would come along with them, so often there would be three carloads full of people making the trip from Cleveland.

Dr. Livshin, an ear, nose, and throat specialist who was a close friend of mine, would perform the operations in his office in the University Building in downtown Syracuse. He had his own surgical room and, next door, a recovery room containing eight cribs for his patients. Over the years, he developed a large tonsillectomy practice from referrals, run strictly on a cash basis. Generalists like myself would come there with their patients and give the anesthetics (generally starting with ethyl chloride and switching to ether) while Dr. Livshin operated. By the time the patient had taken several deep breaths (often while crying) he or she would be relaxed enough for Dr. Livshin to remove the tonsils and the adenoids. Then he would suture the tonsillar fossa (the bed of the enucleated tonsils) and put pressure on the back of the throat to control the bleeding from the adenoid area; usually the whole process took only five to ten minutes. Often, Dr. Livshin would operate on three or four patients in half an hour. His fee was $40 or $50 per patient, $15 of which he would pay the generalist who gave the anesthetic.

As a rule, I would leave my office with my patients about

A LITTLE HELP FROM MY COLLEAGUES

7:00 A.M. and be back by about 10:00 A.M. The trip there and back was about sixty-five miles; the entire trip took about three hours, and my average fee amounted to between $45 and $60. The parents generally remained in Syracuse with their children, taking them home one by one as they recovered.

Dr. Livshin developed a successful practice in Syracuse, but money was not his primary motive. I remember one occasion that illustrates this clearly. I was treating a poor family with three children, male twins five years old and their seven-year-old sister. All three children were constantly sick with tonsillitis and ear infections. Finally, I recommended tonsillectomies for all three of them and told the mother that the fee would be $25. Naturally, I meant the fee would be $25 for each child.

I had called Dr. Livshin earlier to ask him if he would accept this fee. I told him of the family's poor financial plight and told him that I would charge only $10 for giving the anesthetic if he would agree to charge only $25 per child. He agreed, and I drove the children into Syracuse to his office.

As we were preparing them for surgery, the children's mother handed Dr. Livshin $25 in cash, saying that was the fee I had quoted her. I then realized that she had misunderstood me, believing the $25 fee I had quoted covered tonsillectomies for all the children! I was quite embarrassed, but Dr. Livshin shrugged and laughed. "All right, Marv," he said, "as long as the kids are here, let's do the work. I'll take $15 and give you the rest." So we went ahead. Three children got their tonsils out for a total fee of $25, including transportation into Syracuse. Their operations were among the cheapest I ever assisted at!

As the years went by, and younger doctors began to replace the generation with whom I worked so closely, I saw less of Dr. Livshin's kind of humanity and generosity. At the Oneida City Hospital many of the physicians and surgeons who joined the staff after World War II seemed impatient with questions and much less willing to help out either me or my patients. When I would call to say patients were on their way in to the hospital, many were reluctant to accept or treat them on my say-so. There was one physician who was especially difficult to deal with. He seemed to insult my medical skill, embarrassing me and making me feel like a novice whenever I called him to ask him to admit one of my patients. Furthermore, he was rude and often outright mean to my patients themselves. I also found that many of the younger surgeons would not even contact me to inform me of their post-operative findings on patients I sent in. On many occasions, I learned the outcome of a case from the patient's friends or relatives instead of from the surgeon. I found this embarrassing and frustrating.

Moreover, in the 1970s, I found that many of my patients had definite hospital allegiances of their own. Up to that time, I generally had about eight patients hospitalized at the Oneida City Hospital at any given time. But slowly I found that many of my patients to the east preferred to go to the Rome City Hospital, and many of those to the west wished to go to the Syracuse hospitals. These things, combined with my loss of rapport with the staff at the Oneida City Hospital, led to my slow withdrawal from Oneida, until I had only the occasional case there. I continued to visit the Oneida City Hospital but only to attend meetings there of the Madison County Medical Society.

I often recall, however, the warm fellowship of those earlier days at the Oneida City Hospital, when we all seemed to be working together to give the best possible care to our patients. I was privileged to be part of a medical community in the true sense. I will never forget the kindness of Drs. Preston, Freshman, Beach, and many others, or the lessons they taught me in medicine and humanity.

Six
Family Affairs

As the 1930s passed and we entered the decade of the 1940s, my practice grew fast, keeping me busy every day. At home, things were changing too. By early 1939, our son Neal had become an active little boy, interested in everything and everyone around him. When he was seven months old, he brought one of the disadvantages of our home/office arrangement home to us by giving us a good scare.

A young minister had brought his two-year-old son into the office about 10:00 one morning to see me about a persistent cough. Since I was out making house calls, he decided to wait. Bee was doing housework, and the door between the office and our living room had been left open. Naturally the two little boys gravitated toward each other like magnets. When I returned home they were romping together on the floor.

The minister told me his son had had a bad cough for some time. "I'm afraid it might be whooping cough, Doctor Brown," he added. He was so right. It was whooping cough, and naturally Neal caught it.

From whooping cough, Neal progressed to pneumonitis. He had a temperature of 103 degrees with a respiratory rate of between forty and sixty. He wouldn't eat or drink and was very restless. Moreover, his terrible cough kept him from sleeping.

HOUSE CALLS

I began to get pretty worried.

Antibiotics were not available, so I tried the current treatments. I rigged up a croup tent with steam vapor; we forced fluids down our miserable little boy whenever we could, and we tried to get aspirin and some cough expectorant down his throat too. I also gave him nembutal capsules (a common sedative) rectally to make sure he got some sleep, pulling adult capsules apart, and pouring out most of the powder, then pricking the gelatin capsules with a pin to allow the remaining small dose to be slowly released. To our great relief, this sedation allowed Neal to get the sleep he needed to fight off the infection in his lungs. After a few days our son was up and playing as usual.

Our second son was born on December 14, 1940. We named him Miner after Bee's father. His birth soon gave Neal a playmate—and also increased the demands on Bee's busy schedule. Our family was very happy, however, with Bee's laughter at our sons' antics filling our little Cape Cod house.

During the warm days of summer, Bee would walk Neal and Miner down the block toward the Catholic church and parsonage where Father Bulter worked and lived, Neal toddling at her side and Miner in his stroller. Often Father Butler would be out on his lawn, planting flowers or digging weeds, and he and Bee would stop to pass the time of day. Once, when Neal was about three years old, he suddenly looked up, pointed to the sculptured fresco of Christ over the entrance, and piped, "Look, Mommy, Mickey Moose!" A mixed expression came over Father Butler's face, but he took it in good part, and soon became used to Neal's visits to the church.

On Sunday mornings, Neal would often walk to the church on his own, waiting for Mass to conclude. He would slip into the cool vestry and wait for Kathleen Houser, who sometimes helped Bee with the housework and the boys' care. When she appeared, he would take her hand, and they would return to our house together. Once as Neal, Bee, and Miner were on another of their walks, Neal stopped and kissed a large rock in a lawn near the rectory. "Mommy, Blarney Stone," he said. Father Butler, out pruning bushes around the parsonage, got quite a kick out of Neal's action.

"You'd better watch out for this youngster, Mrs. Brown," he said. "If he continues his Sunday morning habits, we'll make a Catholic out of him."

"Well, Father Butler," Bee flashed back, "I would rather have him grow up to be a good Catholic than a poor Jew." Father Butler roared, and, we were told, quoted the incident many times from his pulpit.

On June 3, 1943, our third son, Terry, was ushered into the world. It was a Thursday, our day off, and my nurse/office aide Hoopey was there to watch our boys while Bee and I drove into Syracuse. Bee was having irregular contractions, but we knew that real labor couldn't be far off, so she packed her bag to be ready to go to the hospital if necessary.

Just as we were ready to leave the house, I got a telephone call from Thomas Cox, the Oneida County Coroner, who lived in Rome. He told me that a man had committed suicide in North Bay and asked me, in my capacity as coroner's physician, to pronounce him dead and see to the disposal of the body. I hesitated but, as Bee's contractions were still irregular, finally agreed to go there on our way into Syracuse.

We drove to a farm about a half-mile north of North Bay, and Bee waited in the car while I investigated. I found a male about sixty years old hanging by the neck in the barn. A neighbor had found him and called for help. The state police had arrived just as we did; they cut the body down under my direction. I pronounced the victim dead, phoned Tom Cox with my findings, and released the body to the family's undertaker. All this time Bee was waiting for me, having irregular labor pains.

When we got to Syracuse, it was about 12:30, and Bee was hungry. We went to the College Inn, a favorite restaurant of ours where I would often meet professional colleagues. As we sat down, who should spot us but Bee's obstetrician, Dr.

77

HOUSE CALLS

Morris Schoenwald. When we told him she was having irregular pains, he got excited and urged Bee to come to his office for an examination as soon as we finished lunch. Bee wasn't worried, however. She said that if she started active labor, the hospital would contact him.

By the end of our lunch, the pains were getting harder, and I wanted to take Bee directly to the old General Hospital. Bee refused. She said she had to go to the Wells & Coverly department store in downtown Syracuse to get some underwear for Neal and Miner. A saleslady there had called Bee the day before and told her that a new shipment of children's wear had come in. Since this was during the war years, when supplies were uncertain, Bee was determined to get the things she needed before they disappeared.

Luckily, I found a parking space right in front of the store and waited with the motor running, just in case. It seemed a long time before Bee came out of the store, but she waved her purchases happily. Finally, I was allowed to drive her to the hospital. Terry was born six hours later, at 9:30 P.M. Six years into our marriage, Bee and I had become the parents of three healthy, vigorous boys. Our lives and duties were expanding quickly.

The decade of the forties seemed to fly by. I was on the go constantly, covering my office, making my house calls and hospital visits, and fulfilling my community duties. But Bee, too, had a busy pace to keep up. Three active little boys are enough to keep anyone occupied, but Bee was also running our home, answering the telephone and helping out in my office, and performing the social duties required of the doctor's wife in a small community.

When Terry was three months old, we were both so exhausted that we decided we had to get away from our routine for a few days before we simply collapsed. Bee's mother and Hoopey came to the rescue. They packed us off to the Adirondack Mountains for Labor Day weekend, assuring us that they had everything under control. I remember that on our first day at the Brown Swan resort, Bee and I came down only for meals, spending the rest of the day making up for lost sleep. When we finally emerged from hibernation, our fellow guests greeted us with catcalls and suggestive sallies. They had decided that we were honeymooners! Only documentary evidence—a picture of our three sons—convinced them otherwise. That long weekend was a life-saver. We returned to Cleveland rested, refreshed, and ready to resume our busy lives.

During those early years, getting away even for a few short days was difficult for Bee and me. Usually our holidays were combined with medical meetings or other learning experiences. Every year for about ten years, we would get away in June for the New York State Health Officers' convention, held at first in Saratoga Springs, and later in Lake Placid. Later in the year, generally in October, Bee and her Eastern Star sisters would attend the state meeting in New York City. I would then join Bee there for a long weekend.

Hoopey usually acted as our stand-in for such excursions, managing our home and office with the loving care of a member of the family. Sometimes she would also take over for special holidays. In 1945, for instance, she filled in when Bee and I took off for a special five-day vacation in the Adirondacks to celebrate our eighth wedding anniversary. As we left on this much-needed trip, Hoopey presented us with a poem she had written in honor of the occasion. It shows the strength of bond we had with her, and we have cherished it ever since:

June 20, 1945

For: Beatrice and Marvin Brown
On: Honeymoon Trip #9
Via: Married Life Express
To: The State of Bliss—Forever

I didn't get a fancy card—didn't even try
There's just some gabby sweet talk on every card you buy.
Of course, I wish you Happiness and Friends both old and new

HOUSE CALLS

    And Health and Wealth and grandchildren—when Time
        makes them come due.
    And I'm very glad you married and raised a family
    Because if you just hadn't—there would be no place for me.
    But hidden faults and weaknesses sometimes cause folks to part
    And to prevent that—I'll confess—the sin that's in my heart
    I'm Jealous—
        Jealous of the very fact that Fate put us together
        (and bound and determined to stay put in spite of
            wind or weather).
        Jealous of the confidence in me you have displayed
        (and cross my heart and hope to die if ever it's betrayed).
        Jealous of the shoulder I can laugh or cry upon
        (and proud to be the cushion for your life as we go on).
        Jealous of the Happiness with which your home is filled
        (and anyone who'd mess it up is likely to get killed).
        Jealous of the fervent kiss the boys give me at night
        (no matter what the day has brought that kiss
            makes it all right).
        Jealous of your deep true love, that shines through
            all you do
        (and want to see it start each day to blossom out anew).
    There, now you know the dreadful Thoughts that fill
        my waking hours
    Can realize how deep I've sunk in Dark and Awful Powers
    But yet I hope that you'll forgive and with you I'll remain
    And be the Mama and the Nurse each time you
        board this train.

                                              With Love,
                                              Hoopey

    The holidays that Hoopey's loving aid allowed us recharged us for our busy lives. We needed a break once in a while, but we also loved our boys and our daily activities.

    Both Bee and I took great pleasure in watching our boys grow and develop. We shared with all parents the complaint that they were growing up too fast, developing, almost before we know it, lives and interests of their own.

FAMILY AFFAIRS

Miner was our outdoor boy. Even in his pre-kindergarten days he would spend most of his time playing outside, no matter what the weather. On cold winter days, Bee would hang on to an impatient, wiggling Miner, dressing him in layer after layer of clothes and finally releasing him to his beloved outdoors. He would cross the street, accompanied by his constant companion, a cocker spaniel named Lady, and head for the frozen lake, where boy and dog, the one fatly wrapped in hat and coat, scarves and mittens, and the other bounding with ears flying, would slide and roll in the snow for hours. Bee, from our front window, would check frequently on the pair, two small shapes dark against the white expanse. When he had had enough, Miner would troop back home, covered in snow, with cheeks and nose glowing. "Where were you today, Miner?" I would ask when I got home. "I was on the yake with Yady," he would reply happily.

Summer yielded other pleasures to our boys. There was a wooded lot bounding the lake, about half a block to our west, that became a favorite summer haunt. There the boys would go to skip stones on the surface of the water and watch the life around them: the water snakes whose sleek heads would appear near the shoreline, the fish leaping further out. It was a great place for them to learn some of nature's secrets.

One warm summer's day Miner, then three and a half, went to this lot with Lady and some of his playmates. When the children had had their fill of playing, they started for home, walking single file along the lakeshore highway. They had been told to walk on the gravel shoulder, but the smooth pavement of the highway itself was too tempting; they began walking on its edge. Suddenly a large truck came zooming toward them around a bend, directly in line with Miner, who was leading. Lady leaped at Miner, pushing him off the highway onto the shoulder. The next moment, the truck struck Lady full in the body, killing her instantly.

The children were horrified. Miner ran home as fast as he could. Tears streaming down his cheeks, he confronted Bee.

HOUSE CALLS

"What's the matter with Yady? She's lying along the side of the road, and blood is coming out of her mouth." The other children came up, and Bee soon learned what had happened. She called Hoopey's father, Papa Neal, and he brought Lady's body to his house. The next day, Lady was buried there, beneath an apple tree, with Papa Neal officiating at the funeral and a crew of doleful children acting as mourners.

Lady's death saddened us all, but for a while, at least, Bee and I were more haunted by the thought that Miner had so nearly been the victim of the charging truck. Lady had saved our son at the cost of her own life. In time, however, our grief and fear faded, and a new cocker spaniel, Cindy, joined our household. Miner never formed the attachment for Cindy that he had had for Lady, but Cindy did become a beloved part of the family, sharing our lives for fifteen years.

Miner's love of the outdoors never diminished. One of his early heroes was our handyman, Frank Green. Frank was a slim, muscular man with graying brown hair and a ruddy, weathered face. When he laughed or smiled—a frequent occurrence—his single upper tooth stood out like a beacon. He had served in the army during World War I and often wore his army fatigues when he came over to work for us. Frank could fix anything. It seemed he was always around, painting, repairing a lawn mower, pouring concrete to hold in the supports for an outside clothesline. But he won Miner's heart by his skill as a gardener. When we moved to a bigger house in 1947, Frank planted fifty poplars along the western border of our lot. He landscaped and planted the first shrubs in front of our new office wing. He seeded our lawn and started the rose garden which for years was Bee's favorite spot. Each spring, Bee, Frank, and I would pour over flower catalogues together, choosing the plants to be added that year. And in all these enterprises, Miner was Frank's shadow and helper. Frank helped us in countless ways over the years, but I'll always be most grateful to him for his kindness to the small boy who trooped at his side as he worked in the garden. Miner doubtless got in Frank's way and slowed his labors at times, but Frank never let Miner suspect that he was anything other than a great help. From Frank's example, all our boys, but especially Miner, learned the patient attention to detail that leads to excellent results in any endeavor.

Miner was our champion outdoorsman, but all our boys loved camping. Our family was introduced to camping by Aaron and Lillian Rose. Aaron and Lillian were leaders in the Syracuse Jewish community. Aaron also served as the director of the summer camp for the Syracuse Jewish children called Bradley Brook Camp. Neal, at the age of six, had his first experience with camping there. But in 1945, Aaron and Lillian decided to strike out on their own. They bought a camp in Franklin County, New York, on upper Lake Chateaugay, and opened it the next July. Aaron asked a number of physician friends of his, including me, to serve in turn during the summer months as camp doctor. By chance, I served as the camp's first doctor. Bee, the boys, and I drove up a few days before camp opened and settled into the main house with other staff members. We had a bedroom with a large, screened-in veranda adjoining; it wasn't the Hotel Syracuse, but for a camp, the accommodations were first class.

I took two weeks off from my practice—the first long vacation I had had since I came to Cleveland—and the five of us settled down for a real family holiday. We boated and hiked, ate and relaxed. It was wonderful. My duties as camp doctor seemed very light compared to my practice, although I do remember being asked to pitch in and help dig a cesspool! The boys—even three-year-old Terry—enjoyed themselves as much as Bee and I did. Every morning at about five o'clock, when the sunlight began to sift through the mist covering the lake, I would hear the patter of footsteps heading off down the hall to the bunk of the waterfront counselor, Paul McCabe. It was Terry, ready to pull the sleepy Paul off to the lake for their customary early morning row. Occasionally we would catch the sound of their oars plunking into the quiet lake, or, peering from our warm bed, catch a glimpse of the pair through threads of clearing mist. Terry loved the special attention Paul gave him.

For many years thereafter, I served a two-week stint as Camp Chateaugay's doctor in July. Bee and the boys always came with me, giving us a family-style vacation that otherwise was rare in our lives.

Miner, unlike our other boys, never attended Camp Chateaugay as a camper, however. His love of camping led him into scouting; at that point he decided that Camp Chateaugay was too modern and tame for him, and he went instead to the Oswego County Boy Scout camp, Camp Twelve Pines. He was there first as a camper and later as the waterfront counselor. In time, he became the first Eagle Scout in the Cleveland area.

While Miner was exploring the outdoors, Neal was launching into the pleasures of school and friends. One of his closest friends was a schoolmate named Earl Mangus. When Neal was about eight years old, he and Earl were inseparable. If Neal wasn't in sight, we could safely bet he was at Earl's.

One day, the two boys had disappeared for a time, when suddenly Neal dashed into our house, out of breath and red in the face. He had run all the way from Earl's house on Center Street, a distance of about half a mile. He burst into the kitchen, where Bee was working, and exclaimed, "It wasn't my rock that broke the window."

Such statements tend to strike dread into the hearts of parents. Bee immediately called Mrs. Mangus to find out what had happened. "It's all right, Bee," Mrs. Mangus said. "Neal's quite right. The kids were playing ball, and Earl missed his mark and broke a cellar window. Neal's not to blame at all."

Neal, a little on his dignity, remarked to his now sympathetic mother, "See Mom, I told the truth."

The source of misunderstanding between adults and children is not always so clear-cut, however. Often, the two groups view the world from very different—and mutually confusing—

perspectives. I remember one occasion when Neal and Miner seriously alarmed their babysitter, Emma Dwyer, without in the least intending to. Emma, an elderly lady devoted to our boys, had become their regular babysitter on our Thursdays off. One Thursday afternoon in early July, the year Neal was ten, he and Miner asked Emma if they could go berrying with their friends, Leo and Peter Bitz. Emma agreed, and the foursome set off. Anyone who has gone berrying knows how easily the time slips away in pursuit of the plumpest berry. But for Emma, waiting at the house, the afternoon passed slowly, and the boys didn't reappear. The long summer evening set in; five o'clock passed, then six, and seven was approaching. Emma's state of mind had progressed from mild irritation to worry to real fear. Just as she was about to call for help in finding the boys, they appeared with full baskets, hot, dirty, cheerful, and completely unaware of the anxious time they had given Emma.

"Do you know how late it is?" she scolded them. "Do you know it's past suppertime? How could you stay out so late? I didn't have the least idea where you were or where I should start looking!"

The boys were really sorry to have upset Emma. But Neal, with irrefutable ten-year-old logic, stemmed the flow. "But, Emma," he said earnestly, "you didn't have to worry. We knew where we were!"

Neal was also launching into school at this time. He was a good student and seemed at home with his classmates. A teacher named Anne Welch may have had something to do with his eager attitude. All Cleveland soon came to know and respect Anne's magic gift with children.

Anne was an excellent teacher who had returned to Cleveland, her hometown, to care for her father after her mother died. She inspired good students with her enthusiasm and spent many after-school hours patiently tutoring the slower ones. But she also had a rarer quality: an unending supply of love and compassion for all children. In an era when many children arrived

HOUSE CALLS

at school inadequately clothed and fed, Anne quietly set about remedying their lacks. Long before a government school lunch program had been thought of, Anne set about feeding her hungry students. With her own money, she bought cutlery, dishes, and a refrigerator for the school. She kept the refrigerator stocked with food and cheerfully fed the poorer children nourishing lunches and even breakfasts—often their only substantial meals of the day. During the cold days of winter, she would come early to get the fires going so that the children would arrive to find a warm building. She hunted up clothing for the many children whose parents were unable to provide them with adequate shoes or coats for winter weather, and she also provided the less tangible, but equally real, necessities of comfort, love, and encouragement.

Like most of her students, Neal loved Anne Welch. He soon became one of her helpers, often rising and setting out for school early to help her make sandwiches for lunches or pass out breakfasts of cereal and milk to his hungrier school fellows. Anne taught Neal reading and math, social studies and science, but she also gave him valuable lessons in compassion.

Another of Neal's favorite grownups during his school days was Max Whipple, the school bus driver. My first home delivery in Cleveland, in 1938, had been of Max's daughter, whom he named Beatrice, after my wife. Max was a thin, wiry man of medium height, with sharp features and a ready smile. He loved kidding people and delighted his young passengers with his humor. Neal loved him and would often regale us in the evening with tales of Max's jokes.

As our boys grew and my practice expanded, our little Cape Cod house seemed to shrink. Much as we loved it, Bee and I finally decided that we had to have more room. We talked about enlarging our home, but decided in the end to build a new one instead. Our decision was clinched by the news that Marion Morenus, the eccentric antique dealer, wanted to sell a large building lot just one block west of where we were living.

Bee and I went to look at it and fell in love with it at once. It was a large lot of almost two acres, thickly wooded with oaks, maples, and elms. But best of all, it sloped gently toward Oneida Lake and, crossing the lakeshore highway, included 220 feet of lake frontage. Marion was asking $1,200 for it; I paid the price in twelve monthly installments of $100 each.

With our land chosen, we began looking around for an architect. At this point, Aaron and Lillian Rose told us of a brilliant young Syracuse architect, Willard Smith, who had begun making a fine name for himself in the area. Bee and I looked at some of the houses he had designed and were impressed. Soon afterward, we contacted him, and he agreed to build a new home/office complex on the lot we had bought.

We began to meet with Willard in early 1946. We talked and he drew, sketching this plan and that to get our reaction. However, what began as a warm relationship soon cooled. Willard would make appointments with us—often for late in the evening—and then fail to be there when we arrived. He was hard to contact even by phone—and the months were slipping by. When, in early 1947, we sold our Cape Cod house for $10,000, the pressure was on to get the new house built. The news that Bee was pregnant with our fourth child gave yet more urgency to the project.

However, Willard continued to be most elusive—and when we could catch him, he had only sketches to show us, never blueprints. Upon Willard's assurance that the building would begin very soon, I hired a tree surgeon to cut down selected trees to clear our view of the lake and open up the lot for construction. Finally, the day appointed by Willard for breaking ground arrived: the first Monday in April 1947. He had asked me to hire a crew of two men and a bulldozer and have them ready to begin under his direction at 8:00 A.M. The crew arrived, I arrived—but Willard did not. The men and the bulldozer waited all day, but he never appeared. They came back the next day and waited again. No Willard. Meanwhile, all my frantic efforts to locate him yielded nothing. I dismissed and paid off the crew and grimly continued trying to find Willard. I finally reached him by telephone on the third day. Bee and I together told him in no uncertain terms that we had had enough. We wanted nothing more to do with Willard Smith.

By this time, we had been trying to get a house built for almost fifteen months. We had sketches and a general idea of the layout we wanted, but no measurements and no blueprints. We turned Willard's sketches over to our new architect, Howard Yates, with hope but little confidence. Howard Yates was quite different from Willard Smith, however. Within two weeks, we had complete blueprints, a layout of the property, and sketches of various views of the house in our hands! At last, things were moving.

Yates' plans filled us with excitement. The house he designed was to be spacious and beautifully proportioned, with five bedrooms, a screened-in porch, and lots of storage and work space. It was to have a new method of heating, too: radiant heating, with hot water circulating through copper pipes imbedded in the concrete slab on which the house was to stand. Moreover, it was to have big, well-insulated windows looking south over the lake. My work area was to be equally luxurious, containing a big waiting-room, my private office, four examining rooms (one to be equipped with an X-ray machine), a storage room for the drugs I dispensed, and a half-bathroom. There was even to be a large parking lot for my patients' cars.

By May 1947, work on the house had begun. The building went fast—but Bee's pregnancy seemed to progress even faster. On August 21, 1947, our fourth and last son, Stephen, was born. Once again, Bee had produced a beautiful, healthy little boy. By the time she had recuperated from his birth, the new house was ready to decorate. Soon Bee was immersed in details of paints and wallpaper, carpets and drapes. On December 8, 1947, nearly two years after we had begun the process, we finally moved into our new home. It was a happy day for us all.

FAMILY AFFAIRS

With more room and more storage space simplifying her housekeeping, Bee had more time to give to our sons—and their ever-growing circle of friends. Sometimes it seemed that we had, not four sons, but a dozen-odd children darting about in our house and yard. This never upset Bee; she happily became a second mother to half of Cleveland's children. Bee's patience with and pleasure in our boys was remarkable. One of the drawbacks of my chosen profession was that I had very limited time to spend with my family. But Bee, without complaint, stood in my place when I had to be absent, acting at times as both mother and father to our sons.

Mainly because of our four boys, we bought a new car for Bee's use in 1949—a big Buick station wagon with a sleek wooden body. It was the first car that Bee had ever had for herself, and how she loved it! How the neighborhood loved it, too! Besides taking our boys to Syracuse for religious classes every weekend, Bee used it to transport hoards of children to Boy Scout affairs, school events, or, best of all, to the Saturday night movies shown each week in the Constantia Fire Hall.

On these movie nights, as many as fifteen youngsters would pile into the station wagon, giggling and squirming, for the trip to Constantia. On one such Saturday trip, ten-year-old Neal, sitting in the front next to Bee, turned on the car radio. A Syracuse University basketball game was just beginning, so the national anthem rolled out over the airways.

Neal turned to the crowd of kids bunched in the back, "What's the matter with you? Don't you know you have to stand up when the *Star Spangled Banner* is played?" At once the tangled heap of kids in the back began to writhe, separating into a dozen or so separate kids, all trying to stand up in the moving car. A lot of giggling and several bumped heads resulted before Bee managed to restore order, but no one was seriously hurt. These days, seat belt and child car-seat laws forbid such expeditions on grounds of safety; but our boys look back on those trips with Bee very fondly.

HOUSE CALLS

Neal was not the only sociable one among our boys. Terry also loved company—especially female company. From the time he could toddle, Terry was the family lady-killer. He had an enduring fascination with the opposite sex. In 1949, his special friend was a neighbor girl, whom Terry always referred to by her full name, spoken as one word: JudyAnnSearles.

As Terry's sixth birthday approached, he begged for a full-scale party. Asked by Bee to name the friends he wanted invited, he came up with a list of twenty-five children, headed, of course, by JudyAnnSearles.

The day arrived. Twenty-five lively children, each accompanied by a parent, duly gathered at our new house. By great luck, the day was fine and warm, so Bee was able to let the children onto the grounds while she and some of the other parents prepared things inside. The children were called in to watch Terry open his presents, and then they dispersed again while Bee got ready to serve the ice cream and cake. When all was ready, the kids were gathered—but no Terry was to be found. Suspiciously, JudyAnnSearles was also missing. Leaving Neal in charge, Bee dashed three houses down to the Searles' home. Sure enough, calmly playing with some of his new toys, were Terry and Judy Ann! We teased Terry for years about the day he invited twenty-five children to his party and left them all for JudyAnnSearles.

During these years, Stephen, too, grew quickly, changing from a sturdy toddler to a sweet but strong-willed little boy. He had three older brothers to live up to, and he was determined to keep up.

Stephen had his fifth birthday party only two weeks before a new elementary school, built to replace the old school where Anne Welch had taught, opened its doors for the first time. This new school had no kindergarten, so we planned to keep Stephen at home for one more year before introducing him to the new centralized school system. Stephen, however, had other ideas. He was determined to take his place as a student in the first grade.

Accordingly, on the first day of school, he presented himself in our bedroom at 5 o'clock in the morning, fully dressed in his best clothes. "I'm ready for school," he announced. "When should I leave?"

Bee pulled him close, and we tried to explain why it wasn't a school day for him. "Stephen, we know you want to go to school, and we're proud of you for it," Bee began, "but, honey, there's no class for children your age. All the others will be older."

"You wouldn't want to go to school with nobody but older kids, would you?" I asked.

"Next year all your friends will be going. It will be more fun if you wait," Bee added persuasively.

We thought we had reached an understanding with Stephen. But after breakfast, he disappeared. Soon after, we got a call from Zaida Wise, the first grade teacher at the new school. Apparently Stephen had calmly walked to school and placed himself firmly in the first seat in the first grade classroom.

We had discussed Stephen's desire to start school with Zaida earlier, and she had agreed with us that he was too young. However, when faced with his *fait accompli*, she suggested a compromise. "I hate to squelch such enthusiasm," she said. "What if we let Stephen continue to come informally? He can join in, but I won't enroll him as a permanent student." We agreed, sure that Stephen's interest would fade quickly.

Day after day, however, Stephen continued to get himself up and present himself at school. Moreover, he seemed to have no trouble keeping up with the first grade schoolwork. Finally, we gave in. So at the age of five, Stephen was formally enrolled as a student in the first grade.

Stephen's love of learning continued to grow, but over the next two years, his comparative youth did begin to handicap him. By the time he finished third grade, we decided, with his agreement, to keep him back for a year to allow him to rejoin his own age group; his contentment in the following years proved this decision to be the right one. Despite this later step, however, I will never forget Stephen's proud, determined little face that early morning.

As our sons grew from babyhood to boyhood, our family life presented us with many problems and challenges. But those years also gave Bee and me the immeasurable rewards of parenthood: interest, delight, laughter, pride, and love. They were good years, years that yielded us a rich harvest of memories, and a loving, enduring relationship with our boys.

Seven
The War Years

The 1940s were years of hard work and swift change for me and for Bee; an expanding practice and a growing family kept us both very busy. But along with the pressing concerns of our daily lives, we were soon caught up in larger concerns; the coming of the Second World War stirred even the backwaters of Cleveland.

At first, news of Hitler's rise in Germany seemed to have little to do with us—events in a nation I had never seen. But slowly, accounts began to filter in of a growing persecution of Germany's Jews: curtailment of their rights as citizens, confiscation of property, even imprisonment and physical attacks. The news that, once again, Jews had been singled out for harassment was disturbing. And as Hitler's armies began marching across Europe, our disquiet grew.

By early 1941, refugees from the European war had begun arriving in New York, among them many German and Polish Jewish physicians. The Jewish Placement Agency rose to the occasion. Ways were found to determine these doctors' professional capabilities. Temporary and then permanent medical licenses were issued to them and communities found eager for their services.

One such refugee was Dr. Fritz Schaal. A German Jew, he

had been born and raised in upper Silesia. As a young man, he had attended medical school in Munich and Berlin, completing his education and clinical work in Breslau. There he had met his future wife, Katie, and the two had dreamed of a life there together.

This was 1938, however, and the Nazis were growing strong in Germany. Fritz soon decided that he had no future in a Nazi Germany; he left for the United States, hoping to establish himself and make a home there for Katie. Once in New York City he took out citizenship papers, and studied for and passed medical exams qualifying him to practice medicine in New York State. Meanwhile, things were growing ever worse for Jews in Germany. On November 8, 1938, a German Jew in Paris, enraged by news of his family's expulsion from Germany, headed to the Polish border—along with eighteen thousand other Jews beaten and stripped of their possessions by the SS—and shot a German embassy official. When the official died the next day, Germany exploded into an orgy of anti-Jewish violence. For twenty-four hours, Nazi thugs all over Germany destroyed Jewish homes and shops and attacked their owners. Through the long night, Nazi stormtroops smashed and burned 191 synagogues. So much glass was broken that the Nazis christened the occasion *Kristallnacht*, night of broken glass.

Katie lived through that terrible night in Breslau and decided that she could delay her departure no longer; it was time for all Jews who could leave Germany to do so. She managed to get out and made her way to London. There she worked as a char-woman while she waited to be reunited with Fritz. In May 1939, Fritz flew to London, and the two were married. Fritz then returned to New York and found work in a hospital. Nine months later, armed with an affidavit of support for Katie, he was able to bring her to the United States.

Soon after this reunion, the New York division of the National Committee for the Resettlement of Foreign Physicians placed Fritz in the small upstate village of Deansville, New York,

THE WAR YEARS

where he set up a general practice. Fritz and Katie found it hard to settle down there, however; they had trouble making a living, and they found the new culture hard to adjust to. By this time, Fritz had made friends among his fellow doctors. Several of them practiced near Syracuse, and Fritz decided to try to set up a practice near them. Thus the couple came to Constantia, New York, in May 1941.

Bee and I soon became warm friends with the Schaals, and our shared religion strengthened the bond. The story of their escape from Germany brought the war in Europe home to us; Bee and I tried hard to help them settle in. Their early days in Constantia were trying, however, as Fritz worked to establish his practice. Ironically, it was my practice that, in the main, was making the process hard for the Schaals. I had previously been Constantia's nearest doctor, so most of its citizens were already my patients. Dr. Schaal was caring for the overflow or for patients who needed immediate care when I was away.

Seven months after the Schaals arrived, the Japanese bombing of Pearl Harbor brought the United States into the war. America was mobilizing for battle, and recruitment of the medical profession began at a fever pitch. One of my closest friends, Dr. Ernest Freshman, decided to leave his practice in Oneida and join the armed forces. Aware of the struggle Dr. Schaal was having in establishing himself in Constantia, and realizing that Dr. Freshman's departure would leave a gap in Oneida, I arranged for the two men to meet. Soon they had agreed on a mutually satisfactory arrangement; Dr. Freshman entered the armed forces, and Dr. Schaal took over his practice in Oneida for the duration of the war.

The story of the Schaals' escape from Germany brought the war very close for Bee and me; I was glad to have played a small part in helping them to settle into a new life. My own role during the war was an issue I struggled with for some time, however.

When I had graduated from the Syracuse College of Medicine

in June 1936, I was also given a commission as a first lieutenant in the U.S. Army Medical Reserve. My class had been approached about six weeks earlier to sign up for these commissions, and I had thought it the honorable and patriotic thing to do. My family and Bee, then my fiancée, thought otherwise, however. They were relieved when I showed them a provision in my commission stating that "You will not perform the duties of an officer under this appointment until specifically called to active duty by competent orders." At that time, no one thought a war making such active duty necessary was at all likely.

By 1940, however, war had begun in Europe, and an eventual U.S. role had started to seem more possible. At that point, I had a wife, two small sons, and a growing medical practice in which I was the only doctor for approximately four thousand people in an area of more than four hundred square miles. I thought long and hard about what I should do. I talked with Bee, with my family, with my friends. In the end, I decided that my primary duty was to my family and my patients. In February 1941, I wrote to the War Department requesting that the army accept my resignation as a first lieutenant in the Medical Army Reserve. The following month, I received a letter accepting my resignation; I was no longer a member of the armed forces. As it turned out, I had made my decision with little time to spare; after July 1941, no resignations were accepted.

December 7, 1941, is a date few Americans will forget. Just as Americans of my sons' generation can tell you where they were the day President Kennedy was shot, so Americans old enough to remember at all know just what they were doing when the news of the Japanese attack on Pearl Harbor came through.

At 10 A.M. on December 7, 1941, I was applying a cast to Mrs. Best's left leg. She had fallen and fractured the left tibia just below the knee, and, with Bee's help, I was applying a plaster of paris cast to the leg. We had left the door open between my office and our living room, and the radio was on. Suddenly

THE WAR YEARS

we heard the news: The Japanese had bombed Pearl Harbor in a surprise attack. The next day, we listened to President Franklin D. Roosevelt's address to Congress asking for a declaration of war on Japan: "Yesterday, December 7, 1941—a date which will live in infamy—the United States of America was suddenly and deliberately attacked by the naval and air forces of the Empire of Japan. . . ." Congress voted unanimously for war. It had happened at last. The United States had joined the fighting.

Soon the reality of war was hitting home to us in many ways. With war raging in Europe, Africa, and the Pacific, the United States was gearing up as fast as possible, readying its manpower and setting up factories to turn out war materials around the clock. Young men were flocking to volunteer; fifty or so joined up from the North Shore alone those first months. Local draft boards were set up, and criteria for service, and exemption from it, established. Young heads of families were exempt as long as they worked in a war factory. Others were exempt if they held jobs considered vital to domestic operations or to the war effort.

As for myself, with the United States actually at war, I had reconsidered my earlier decision and tried to enlist as a medical officer in the U.S. Army. Now, however, the draft board refused to accept me, stating that I was needed in my local community and that I could join up only if I found a replacement to take over my medical responsibilities at home. At the time, I was the only physician practicing from Central Square on the west to Oneida and Rome on the east, and from Oneida Lake north for more than fifteen miles. No one seemed eager to take over my practice, so I settled down to care for this large area, virtually alone.

To add to my task, Cleveland and the North Shore, along with the rest of the country, was soon put on an emergency war footing. We staged practice blackouts frequently, and I installed blackout curtains in my office so that in an emergency I could continue to work there. I also had secondary darkened headlights installed in my car so it could be driven almost unnoticeably at night. Gasoline was rationed and limits put on traveling for pleasure. I had little trouble getting gasoline, however, since as a doctor I was required to travel in my work. In fact, because my patients' gas was rationed, the number of house calls and home deliveries I had to make rose swiftly.

I had new, war-related duties, too. My office was equipped with two stretchers and a considerable supply of first aid materials—just in case. And I gave first aid courses locally and in the town halls of Vienna and McConnellsville. To spur the community war effort, I also arranged for E. R. Vadeboncoeur, then a well-known Syracuse radio and television commentator, to give an address in Cleveland; despite the gas rationing, a large group turned out for the event.

Local interest in the war news was high. The war correspondents kept us right up with the news on the latest skirmishes. The famous Kaltenborn gave a daily war summary at 8:55 P.M., and Bee and I seldom missed it. Like Americans all over the country, we tried hard to keep track of our friends who were in the fighting. Occasionally we were saddened by news of the death of someone we had known.

In late 1942, however, the violence of war struck much closer to home than we would ever have thought possible, leaving casualties in our area. On December 23, just over a year after the attack on Pearl Harbor, a bartender from nearby Sylvan Beach, Joe O'Toole, killed one person and seriously wounded two others in his own private war.

Joe and Maude O'Toole had been patients of mine almost since I had begun my practice. They lived in the center of the village of Sylvan Beach, across the road from Russell's Danceland and Cocktail Lounge, where Joe worked. The O'Tooles were a childless couple, well-known and well-liked for their community spirit, their kindness to the village young people, and their patriotism.

Less than two miles from the O'Tooles' home, across the

bridge linking Sylvan Beach and the village of Verona Beach, lived Kenneth and Kei Iyenaga, their children, and Kenneth's mother. The Iyenagas were a well-educated and well-respected American family of Japanese descent. They were clearly loyal to the United States; not only was Kei a board member of the local Red Cross chapter, but the family had donated their car to the national scrap metal drive.

Early in the morning of December 23, Joe stopped by Owen's Bar in Sylvan Beach for a drink. The talk among the patrons ran to the war and the attack on Pearl Harbor that had occurred just a year earlier. Soon Joe was holding forth about how awful it was that "the Japs" had killed so many young Americans in that attack.

Exactly what came over this normally mild sixty-four-year-old bartender, no one knows. But at 8:30 that morning, Joe went home, loaded his rifle, and headed for the Iyenagas' house. On the way, he stopped at the Verona Beach Post Office and told the postmistress, Marie Rice, that he was "going to get those Japs." Then he walked down Jug Point Road and banged on the Iyenagas' door.

Kei Iyenaga answered the knock readily; Joe had been by many times before to buy eggs. This time, however, Joe walked into the kitchen, raised his rifle, and began shooting. When he stopped, Kenneth was dead, and Kei and her mother-in-law were critically wounded. The only child at home, Johnny, escaped out the back way.

His revenge accomplished, Joe walked down to the Mooney's grocery store at the head of Jug Point Road and said calmly, "Call the state troopers. I just shot three Japs."

At his trial, Joe was declared insane at the time of the shooting and was sent to Marcy State Hospital, a mental institution. He remained there for about four years, and then, judged harmless by the doctors there, returned to Sylvan Beach. After his return, Joe seemed subdued and remorseful and lived very quietly with his wife until his death at the age of sixty-eight.

HOUSE CALLS

Kei Iyenaga and her mother-in-law also returned to the area after they recovered from their wounds. Their neighbors tried hard to show their sympathy and sorrow at what had happened.

Joe's rampage had shocked the whole area. It was a tragedy for all concerned, and the shock of it sobered many people excited by romantic notions of war.

For most Americans on the "home front," the war was not romantic at all; it meant shortages of goods and labor, worry about loved ones, and often drudgery. For me, the war meant long days and disturbed nights. I was run ragged covering the broad area of my practice. I remember especially one particular Sunday in January 1943. It seemed that everyone in the area had the flu. It was a bitter cold day; the wind was strong and gusty, and dirty snow banks flanked the roads, covered with a thick icy crust. The air was filled with fine hard snow that drifted across the roads, reducing visibility and making the road surface very slippery. My calls started very early in the morning, and I drove all day making house call after house call; back and forth I drove, from Fish Creek on the east to West Monroe on the west, to Camden and Williamstown on the north. I saw more than fifty people in their homes that day—so many patients that I didn't have enough medicines in my bag to treat them all and had to keep stopping in at my office to replenish my supplies. It was after 10:00 P.M. when I finally drove home for the last time, utterly worn out. The day was exceptional in the number of patients I treated, but the pattern of my days was often similar.

It seemed that the war had been going on forever when one day, as I was driving home from treating an emergency case at the Oneida City Hospital, I heard over the car radio that the Allies had landed in Normandy. It was a little after 5:00 A.M. on June 6, 1944. I was tired almost to stupefaction after my long night's work, but the announcement of the landing acted like a tonic. "The Allied armies under the direction of the Supreme Commander, General Dwight D. Eisenhower, have invaded the coast of Europe and are storming ashore on Omaha Beach in Normandy," intoned the reporter. A chill went up my spine. Was this the beginning of victory, or the end? If it's the beginning, let's get on with it, I thought. Please, let peace be near.

As it turned out, the invasion of Normandy was decisive to the war in Europe. The following year, Germany surrendered as the Allied forces swept its troops out of France and Belgium; following the destruction of Hiroshima and Nagasaki in August 1945, Japan also surrendered. The world had survived a second world war, but with wounds that perhaps have still not entirely healed. At long last, we were free to return to our peacetime lives.

Eight
Advances and Changes

In March 1944, tragedy touched my family. My sister, Mae Brown Rowell, died just one day before her thirty-sixth birthday. Mae was four years older than I was, and we had been close in our early years; I often think of the days we spent playing and running together as children.

I write of Mae's death for another reason, however; it illustrates the vast changes that have taken place in the practice of medicine since our youth together. Had Mae been born today, her medical history would have been very different.

Mae's early death had its roots in her childhood. At the age of eleven, she came down with rheumatic fever. There were no specific medications for this illness at the time; she was very sick for several weeks. Our family doctor treated her swollen, painful joints with hot wet packs and prescribed analgesics for pain. During that illness my job was to run to the corner drugstore daily to buy ice cream for her.

Mae gradually recovered from the acute phase of her illness, but it left her with a damaged heart—a vascular defect known as mitral stenosis. From that time on, Mae was given special loving care in our family; each summer she was sent to a special camp to get lots of fresh air; at home she was encouraged to drink lots of milk and eat many fresh eggs. Outside the family, however, Mae's physical fragility seemed to translate into extreme shyness; she was slow to make friends, and I don't remember her having any boyfriends in school. Instead of finishing high school, Mae decided to attend business school. With the skills she learned there she was able to get a good job, but although her life appeared smooth, she often seemed sad and rather lost. Her social life remained limited; she would go out with our older sister, Dorothy, with our mother, or with other women her own age, mainly to the movies or to musical events.

When Mae was in her early thirties, she went to visit our oldest sister, Fannie, and her husband, Gabriel Reeder, in Buffalo, New York. There she met Lee Rovall, a husky, outgoing, industrious steelworker. Lee was a widower; his wife had died not long before of tuberculosis. He and Mae took to each other and were soon engaged; both were ripe for some good living, and we were all very happy for them.

Lee and Mae married in Syracuse and then set up housekeeping in Buffalo. For the first time I could remember, Mae seemed truly happy. She glowed with vitality and was full of plans for the future.

A few months later, in 1943, Mae announced that she was expecting a child. She had not told Lee of her heart problem, and they were both eager for children. At this time, Mae was thirty-five years old and pregnant for the first time; moreover, her mitral stenosis had advanced over the years into a serious heart defect.

When Bee and I first learned of her pregnancy, she was going into her third month. The news alarmed me; the strain of pregnancy could kill Mae. We both talked long and hard with Mae, urging that she have a therapeutic abortion. Mae consulted several other doctors, and they concurred with my opinion. At this point, Mae finally told Lee of her heart condition. He was concerned, but left the decision of whether or not she should continue to carry the child up to her. Despite our advice, Mae decided to go ahead with the pregnancy. She wanted a child of her own very badly. She finally found an obstetrician who told her she was healthy enough to carry the child, giving her the confidence she needed to proceed.

For the next three or four months, Mae's pregnancy seemed to progress quite well. She had the usual complaints of pregnancy, but she kept her weight under control and took medicine to support her heart condition. When she was seven and a half months pregnant, however, disaster struck. While on a visit to Syracuse, Mae's heart began to beat fast and irregularly. She was rushed to the Memorial Hospital there, but died shortly after admission of heart failure following ventricular fibrillation. Her death was so sudden that the hospital staff could not work fast enough to do a Caesarean section; her unborn fetus died with her.

Mae's early death took two lives at once—and left Lee once again a widower. We all grieved at the waste. As I look back, I know that if Mae had been born today, her death could have been averted, and she might well have completed her pregnancy and had a live child in her arms.

First of all, Mae's rheumatic fever would probably never have occurred. We now know that rheumatic heart disease often follows an acute streptococci infection. If penicillin had been available to treat the strep throat that probably led to Mae's attack of rheumatic fever, that illness—and the heart condition it left her with—might not have developed in the first place.

Even if Mae had developed heart disease, however, her diseased mitral valve could today have been replaced by either a man-made valve or a pig valve. Such cardiac surgery did not come into its own, though, until after the heart-lung machine was invented, making it possible to stop the heart from beating while allowing the body's blood to bypass the heart and lungs and continue to supply the rest of the body. These advances were first developed in the late 1950s and early 1960s; they are now routine in most large hospitals.

Finally, even if Mae had become pregnant with her heart

problem unresolved, it is likely that the improved care available now would have allowed her and possibly her unborn child to survive the pregnancy. Mae made it seven and a half months into her pregnancy with little special aid; today she would have had greatly advanced medications and medical technology to help her.

Mae's tragic case illustrates only a few of the medical advances I witnessed over the course of my career. Since I qualified to practice medicine in 1936, there have been huge advances in surgical methods, in medical technology, and in the medications available to treat the sick. There have also been huge changes, perhaps not all for the better, in the delivery of medical care, from the dispensing of medicines to the nature of the doctor-patient relationship, to the cost of care.

Medical technology and surgical techniques have changed drastically since I began practicing medicine. In describing Mae's case, I have already mentioned the advent of the heart-lung machine and the advances it made possible in cardiac surgery. Technological advances have allowed similar dramatic improvements in other kinds of surgery, as well as in diagnosis and in nonsurgical methods of treatment. One of my early experiences at the old Syracuse General Hospital illustrates how far technology has changed since those early days.

When I arrived there as an intern in 1936, abdominal surgery could be a dangerous business. Despite all the care that could be taken, patients often developed complications, including severe infections. Appendicitis victims, especially if the appendix had ruptured before it was removed, were prone to peritonitis. Although sulfa drugs came into use later that year to combat infection, at the time the only treatment for such infections was a regimen of supportive measures—forcing fluids by mouth or as an infusion given intramuscularly, giving analgesics for pain, and giving salicylates to reduce fever—that might or might not work.

However, shortly after my arrival, a fellow intern named

ADVANCES AND CHANGES

Damarjian and I read about a recently invented method of treating the markedly distended abdomens common to abdominal infections. First used by Dr. Wangensteen of the University of Minnesota Medical Hospital in Minneapolis, the procedure involved draining the gastrointestinal tract by negative suction and became known as the Wangensteen drainage.

Dr. Damarjian and I, following instructions in an article in the *Archives of Surgery*, went to the hospital laboratory and constructed the apparatus. We had to heat glass tubing, bend it to form various angles, and then attach an array of corks, rubber hoses, and bottles. The resulting article was distinctly odd-looking—rather like a Rube Goldberg contraption—but we hoped for the best.

We didn't have to wait long to try the apparatus out. That night a middle-aged man came in with a ruptured appendix. He was operated on, and his appendix was removed, but peritonitis had already set in. Despite the best supportive treatment available, by the third post-operative day his abdomen was terribly distended, the skin stretched like a balloon. We decided that it was time to try "our" Wangensteen drainage method.

We went to work with our strange apparatus, sliding a rubber tube intranasally down the oesophagus into the patient's stomach and attaching the loose end to the suction bottle. Our contraption may have looked strange, but it certainly worked! Old gastrointestinal material and gas by the quarts filled our bottles and the distended belly went down and down. In a few days the patient rallied; within two weeks he was well enough to go home and resume his normal life.

The Wangensteen drainage method is still used today and is still saving lives. But the apparatus no longer has to be put together from instructions in a journal article, and the design is much simpler and easier to use.

Surgical and technological developments have saved many lives, but perhaps the most far-reaching medical advance that

HOUSE CALLS

I have lived through is the development of antibiotics for use against infection. Before their advent, often the only treatments for severe infections were supportive measures that often failed. When infection struck, it was a fight to see which was stronger, the invading micro-organism or the inner resources, mental and physical, of the patient.

Sulfa drugs were among the first antibiotics to be put into general use. They were developed in the 1930s following an accidental discovery in 1935 by Dr. Gerhard Domagk in Germany. While doing experimental work with mice in a dye factory, Domagk found that mice infected with streptococci improved dramatically when treated with an orange dye by the trade name of Prontosil. The dye Prontosil was broken down chemically in Paris by a husband and wife team, the Trefonels. They found that it contained an old coal tar chemical, para-amino-benzine-sulfonamide, which is sulfanilamide. It had been synthesized by a man named P. Gelmo for his Ph.D. before World War I, but its application for medicine was not realized, and so it was not developed then. Once the medical significance of the sulfa compounds was understood, Dr. Perrin Long of the Johns Hopkins University brought Prontosil (sulfanilamide) to the United States, where he began using it in clinical medicine in 1936 and 1937.

My first experience with these sulfa drugs was in 1937, when I was interning at the old Syracuse General Hospital. A young man came into the hospital with a severely infected arm. He had injured it at work several days earlier and left it alone, hoping it would heal of its own accord. By the time he came to the hospital, his arm was markedly red, swollen, and tender. A diagnosis of cellulitis (tissue inflammation under the skin) was made, and we discussed how to treat it. We had just reviewed two of the new sulfa medications, Prontosil and Prontolyn, and decided to try them in this case. We gave both of them to the young man—first Prontosil by injection, then Prontolyn by mouth, and waited for results. In four to five days, the man's arm had improved dramatically, and we were able to discharge him. It seemed like a miracle. Without the sulfa drugs, all we could have done for the patient was to pack his arm continuously with hot wet compresses in the hope that the infection would localize so that it could be drained. Instead, simple doses of the sulfa drugs had healed the arm quickly and completely.

My experience with sulfa drugs at the old Syracuse General Hospital encouraged me to use them in private practice. In late 1939, a patient of mine named Arthur Sable became the first person on the North Shore to receive sulfa drugs. Art, the school bus driver for the North Bay district, was a husky man in his early forties. One day, his wife called me to their home, saying that Art had chest pains and a bad cough and was having trouble breathing. When I examined him, I found that he had pneumonia. At that time pneumonia was a serious disease.

When I was a medical student, one of our clinical professors was Dr. Joseph Wiseman. He would tell us that when we were confronted with a case of pneumonia we could tell the family that the patient had a 66.66 percent chance of survival; about 1/3 of the patients died. We students would joke that a good way to die would be to reach the age of sixty-three, get pneumonia, go into a coma, and sleep our lives away.

Some of the old-timers still remember the times when we would sit with a pneumonia patient and wait for the crisis to develop. Given good supportive care—lots of fluids, a soft diet, continual bathing, aspirin, analgesics, and the use of an oxygen tent—this would occur at about the fifth or sixth day of the illness. A successful passage through it was marked by a sudden drop in temperature, a return to normal breathing and pulse, and a deep cough raising large amounts of rusty sputum. Those patients who died usually did so at the crisis point; the ones who survived it went into convalescence, a process of several weeks.

I decided to try a sulfa drug to combat Art's infection quickly. At that time, the three sulfa drugs in common use were sulfa thiazole, sulfapyridine, and sulfanilamide. I had been reading up on the three of them and had decided that sulfapyridine showed better results. It did have two possible serious complications, however; cyanosis (a bluish tint to the skin indicating insufficient oxygen in the blood) and increased respiratory distress.

I started Art with one gram of sulfapyridine every four hours, along with the usual supportive measures: complete bed rest, plenty of fluids, good nursing care, the use of aspirin compounds for pain, and cough syrup when necessary. But because of the possible complications that could result from using the new drug, I kept a close watch on his progress, visiting him at his home twice a day. On the evening of the third day, I was alarmed to find that Art seemed to be developing both complications: his lips and face were markedly bluish, and his breathing was very slow and labored. I told his family that these signs were serious and urged them to take Art to a hospital, but they insisted on keeping him at home. I told them, therefore, not to give Art any more sulfa medication until I saw him the next morning.

I didn't sleep very well that night; I was really worried about Art. He was undoubtedly very sick. However, when I visited him the next morning, the change in his condition was marvelous. He was sitting up, obviously alert, and greeted me with his typical quizzical smile. He was coughing up large amounts of phlegm, his color was much better, and his temperature was normal. I was thrilled; the results of using sulfapyridine had justified the risk. Art had gone through a positive crisis and was going to survive his bout with pneumonia. From that point on, his recovery was rapid; within a few days he was up and about, and a week later he was back on his bus route.

In 1939, however, sulfa drugs were not yet consistently available; another method of treating certain types of pneumococcal pneumonia was in common use instead: anti-pneumococcal serum. There are at least thirty-odd types of pneumococcal pneumonia, and serums had been developed for only a few of them. For Type I pneumococcal pneumonia, however,

ADVANCES AND CHANGES

the serum was very effective.

I recall treating a case of Type I pneumococcal pneumonia with the serum in my second winter in private practice. It was a dramatic case in more ways than one.

About 6:00 P.M. a frantic husband phoned, telling me that his wife was very sick with a range of symptoms that sounded very much like pneumonia: labored breathing, severe attacks of coughing, chest pains, and a high fever. The couple lived in a farmhouse deep in the woods beyond Fish Creek Landing and Sylvan Beach. It had been snowing heavily all day and the road to their house was impassable. It would have been difficult to try to transport the sick woman to a hospital; I had to try to get to her instead.

I called Ralph Wheeler, the supervisor of roads for the Town of Vienna, and explained the situation. He agreed to meet me with a snowplow at 7:30 at Vienna Corners, about twelve miles east of my office on Route 49. When I arrived at the crossroads, Ralph was already waiting for me with the town snowplow. I followed him down into Fish Creek Landing and over a narrow road through the woods to my patient's house. This trip would ordinarily have taken about five minutes; this time it took about an hour of hard driving.

When I arrived, I found that my patient, a heavy-set woman of about thirty-five, did indeed have pneumonia. I got a sample of her sputum and had her sister take it to the Madison County Laboratory for typing. In the meantime I left some cough syrup and analgesics and returned home to wait for the lab results.

About 11:00 P.M., the lab in Oneida called to tell me that my patient had Type I pneumonia and that the patient's sister was on her way home with the serum. So back to the farm I drove, relieved to be able to begin the woman's treatment that night. I injected the necessary amount of serum intravenously and waited to see if any unusual reaction developed. Observing none, I returned home and went to bed.

The next morning at about 10 o'clock, I drove out again

to examine my patient. To my surprise, she was already markedly better and was sitting up with good color. Her fever was gone, the pain in her chest had subsided, and she was coughing up a large amount of sputum and phlegm. Apparently the serum had turned the trick, creating a favorable crisis in the early morning hours.

The anti-pneumococcal serums seemed wonderful to us then, but they were specific to pneumococcal pneumonia only, and then to only Types I and III. Sulfa drugs and the many antibiotics that followed them worked to cure not only pneumococcal pneumonia but also a vast range of infections. To doctors in the late 1930s, the sulfa drugs seemed miraculous, replacing long and uncertain supportive measures with quicker and more effective treatments.

One area in which they saved many lives was that of obstetrics. Before sulfa drugs were available, many mothers still died in or shortly after childbirth from puerperal infections. The infection would travel from the uterus into the bloodstream, resulting in general septicemia and finally death. Sulfa drugs, and later other antibiotics, changed all that. I remember my excitement when, in 1939, I read an article in *The Ladies Home Journal* ("That Mothers May Live" by J. C. Furnas) recounting the dramatic drop in maternal mortality rates in 1937 and 1938, and giving sulfa drugs much of the credit.

Even more dramatic and far-reaching, however, was the rise of penicillin. Of all the great advances in industry, technology, electronics, communications, and medicine over the last fifty years, to me the advent of penicillin was the greatest. It has saved many lives, but it has also performed a less dramatic but equally useful function—making countless people more comfortable by relieving their minor infections. I often wonder now how we doctors ever did without it.

Oddly enough, penicillin was first discovered in 1928, before the sulfa drugs. Like many other great advances, its discovery was accidental. While growing staphylococci bacteria in culture

ADVANCES AND CHANGES

dishes in a London hospital, Dr. Alexander Fleming found that mold had ruined one of his cultures. When he examined the culture closely, he noticed that the mold had produced a clear, bacteria-free liquid area between it and the staphylococci; the mold had killed the staph bacteria adjacent to it. Fleming published his findings the following year. The mold had been named penicillium—from the Latin for "pencil" because of its pencil-like shape—so Fleming named its by-product penicillin.

It took ten years of additional research by others before penicillin was ready to be put to use saving lives. The first patient to be treated with it was a British policeman who was dying of septicemia; he recovered, setting off a new era in medical treatment.

It wasn't long before the production of penicillin was big business. But the war was on; facilities for its production were lacking. For this reason, penicillin was first manufactured on a large scale by the beer industry! The large vats usually used for brewing beer were soon cooking up batches of pencillin instead. At first, though, the penicillin produced was not available for general use; it was commandeered for the armed forces. It wasn't until 1944 that the War Production Board allowed penicillin to be provided for civilians. One thousand hospitals were chosen to be the first in the United States to use the drug to treat their patients. Finally, doctors could treat patients suffering from diseases caused by staphylococci, streptococci, pneumococci, and gonococci, and later from diseases such as syphilis and bacterial endocarditis, with a good outlook for success.

When I first began treating patients with penicillin and observing the results, I was amazed. It was a pleasure to treat patients suffering from pneumonia, strep throat, middle ear infections, cellulitis, scarlet fever, and the many other bacterial infections susceptible to penicillin and to watch their quick recoveries. After years of battling infections with supportive measures alone, it was wonderfully satisfying to have an effective weapon at last.

HOUSE CALLS

At first we got the penicillin in powder form. I would take up some sterile peanut or sesame-seed oil in a syringe and inject it into a bottle of the powder hoping to get the powdered penicillin into the oily solution. Then I would inject this combination into the buttocks of my patient. This method produced cures—but also many sore bottoms and cold abscesses. Later I improved on this method by first injecting sterile water into the powdered soluble penicillin and then injecting this solution into a second bottle of the sterile oil, so that after injecting this combination into the patient's buttocks, a depot was created to disburse the penicillin slowly into the muscle tissue. Sore bottoms and cold abscesses continued, however, until the penicillin became available in a solution form. As the years went by, the purity and refinement of the drug improved, and its success rate improved along with it.

The usual dose at first was 30,000 units every day, or every four hours, depending on the disease. In 1945, the price ranged from about $3 to $10 for 100,000 units. A year earlier, the price was $20 for 100,000 units. Today, it is not uncommon to give a patient millions of units in one day, and the price for a bottle of 10 ml. penicillin containing three million units is about $2.

No drug is infallible, however, and penicillin is no exception. Some patients did react unfavorably, with serious complications. In time, however, researchers found substitutes to treat those who developed serious complications from penicillin. A host of other antibiotics now exist, often specifically designed to treat a particular disease, and new ones are marketed almost daily. Penicillin remains one of the most widely used and widely effective, however. Dr. Fleming once remarked that "it would be strange indeed if the first one described remained the best," but, in fact, penicillin is still one of the best antibiotics: effective and remarkably versatile.

The rise of antibiotics—and especially of penicillin—was one of the most far-reaching advances to occur during my lifetime,

ADVANCES AND CHANGES

but antibiotics were by no means the only important kind of medicines to be developed over the last forty years. Indeed, there has been such an explosion of new medications over that period that it takes hard work for doctors to keep abreast of them.

It is not only the medicines themselves that have changed; their modes of delivery have changed too. When I started my practice in 1938, I dispensed more medicines than I prescribed. This was common practice then among country doctors. In an era when cars were still not universally owned and many roads were still unpaved, the practice of dispensing my own medicines saved my patients many miles of travel to a drugstore; the drugstore nearest to my office was fifteen miles away, and the distance from some of my patients' homes was even greater. It would have made no sense to go to the trouble of making house calls and then expect my patients or their families to go out for the medicine that was needed. This service also saved my patients money; I would usually charge them only what a drug cost me, or a few pennies more. Besides, when I dispensed medicines, the patient could begin treatment immediately.

In the early years, my pharmacopeia was limited but usually adequate for most occasions. When it was not, and a special drug was needed, I would write a prescription; such cases were few, however. I kept my main stock of medications in a drug room in my office and carried a smaller supply of the most commonly needed medicines in the black bag I took with me on home visits.

Among the medicines that filled my shelves at the beginning of my practice were analgesics (painkillers), sedatives, laxatives, cough medicines, heart medicines, and stomach medicines. The painkillers included aspirin compounds, acetaminophen tablets, and H.P.A. tablets (containing hydrocyamus, phenobarbital, and aspirin). For severe pain, I stocked 15 mg. soluble morphine tablets which I dissolved in water (heated in a teaspoon with a match) and then injected. My sedatives included phenobarbital in tablet and liquid form, sugar-coated bromide tablets, and

HOUSE CALLS

nembutal capsules. I used evacugen tablets as a laxative.

For colds and upper respiratory illnesses—common among my patients—I used a combination that became known locally as "Dr. Brown's cold tablets": green aspirin compound tablets together with yellow tablets containing aspirin and Dover's powder, to reduce pain and fever. The heart medicines I used in those early days included whole-leaf digitalis tablets (whole, dried leaves of the foxglove plant ground with a paste into pills of one grain in strength), nitroglycerine tablets, quinidine tablets, and strychnine tablets of 1/60 of a grain; for emergencies I often injected Lanatoside C, a powerful, fast-acting digitalis compound, intravenously and used mercurial diuretics for patients in heart failure. The stomach medicine I most commonly dispensed was simple bicarbonate of soda, flavored with peppermint. I also had an assortment of other medicines: ear drops, nose drops, calamine lotion for itching, massage ointment containing methyl salicylate and methol, Butescin picrate ointment for burns, Whitfield's ointment for athlete's foot, Unguentine ointment for any and all skin wounds, and Syrup of Ipecac to induce vomiting in cases of accidental poisoning. All my pregnant patients were dispensed Natabec capsules, a multivitamin and iron supplement, and I prescribed Massengill powder for douches. For those patients who insisted on a tonic, I dispensed pint bottles of Livitamin (containing vitamins and iron) and elixer of I.Q. and S. (Iron, Quinine, and Strychnine). I often wondered whether the good results obtained from these tonics were due to the medicinal ingredients or to the alcohol which was their vehicle! I also kept a supply of thiamine chloride (B_1 vitamins) as tonic pills. For emergency cases I kept a supply of adrenalin ampules (often life-saving in counteracting asthma attacks and allergic reactions to bee stings, drugs, or other substances); theophylline ampules to counteract asthma and emphysema attacks; and dextrose solution ampules to counteract insulin shock in diabetics.

As the years passed, hundreds of sophisticated and specific drugs were developed so that I was continually discarding medicines, replacing them with others, and adding more to my stock. New analgesics such as the Darvon compounds, Demerol, and Tylenol with codeine; newer sulfa drugs; penicillin and other antibiotics; tranquilizers; and antihypertensives all made their way into my store of drugs. As time went on, I also added antihistamines, birth control pills, specific vaginal creams, and a variety of steroid medicines. Digoxin and digitoxin, more refined forms of digitalis, replaced whole-leaf digitalis tablets in my stock of heart medications; atropine compounds were dropped in favor of newer antispastic medications; and newer antacids took the place of bicarbonate of soda on my shelves.

By the time I retired, almost none of the drugs with which I had begun my practice were still in use; and as cars became universal and roads improved, I began prescribing more and more and dispensing less and less.

Another great change in medical practice over my lifetime has been the growth of preventive medicine. One area which this concept has particularly revolutionized is obstetrics.

When I began my practice, many of the women I delivered never had any prenatal care. The first I would hear of their pregnancies was when a husband or neighbor would call and tell me, "She is having five-minute pains." I was expected to drop whatever I was doing and go deliver the baby. For the first several years in practice, I did this, but after a time I began to refuse maternity cases unless the mother came in throughout her pregnancy for regular monthly checkups. This encouraged my pregnant patients to come in early for care and enabled me to educate them about the needs of their unborn children. Early checkups also helped me to spot abnormalities within the first trimester of a pregnancy.

Prenatal care has changed a good deal over the years. I gave my mothers blood tests in the early years but usually only to rule out syphilis. These days, many sophisticated blood tests are taken routinely, and, if indicated, sonograms (a new method of imaging fetal growth with sound waves) and tests on amniotic fluid are also available, especially to spot genetic defects.

Despite the early years when many mothers ignored the benefits of prenatal care, I have been fortunate in my deliveries. Over my career, I delivered just under fifteen hundred babies, six hundred of them being home deliveries. Out of that total, only fourteen babies were delivered by Caesarean section, and twenty-two were stillborn. Only two of the babies I delivered were severely handicapped, and only two mothers died. One was the mother with a *placenta percreta* whom I delivered at the Syracuse General Hospital in 1937. The other was a mother who refused (for religious reasons) to have a therapeutic abortion despite her severe pre-eclampsia (severe toxemia of pregnancy). She died, but with Dr. Beach's help, a C-section was performed, saving the life of her son, who grew up to be a fine, upright citizen.

Preventive medicine has made great progress in areas other than obstetrics as well. One area in which I was privileged to contribute to this progress was in immunization. As the local doctor, as the school physician, and as the health officer for the township of Constantia, it was my duty to protect the children of the area from communicable diseases. During the early years, I conducted these immunization clinics in my office. At first Bee was my only helper; later my nurse worked with us. Generally I held these clinics on Thursdays, my day off, when the office would be free of patients except for emergency cases. The children of Cleveland would walk down to my office from their school, a distance of about half a mile. The children of Panther Lake were driven to my office from their one-room school, a distance of seven miles, by my friend and patient of many years, Max Whipple, in a twelve-passenger minibus. Kenneth Godfrey, another friend and helper, drove the children of Bernhards Bay and Constantia to and from my office for their shots. Preschool children were brought to the office-clinic by their parents.

When I began my practice, such clinics were something new for the people of the area. I had to work hard to sell the idea

ADVANCES AND CHANGES

to many of the parents; it took a lot of discussion to get some of them to see the value of immunizations for their children.

In those early days, I immunized the children against smallpox, diphtheria, and tetanus. Protection against whooping cough, mumps, measles (both Rubeola and Rubella), and polio came in later. As they did, I made those shots available, too. I remember clearly when the Salk vaccine for polio first came out in the mid-1950s. At that time, polio was still quite prevalent, and parents of small children tended to panic whenever one of their children got sick, especially during the warm days of summer. Assisted by my nurse, Doris Marcellus, and Olive Getman, my senior school nurse, I held one of the first local polio clinics, vaccinating residents up to twenty years of age. The parents were relieved—and so was I. In time the vaccinations slowly cut the number of polio victims, and the reassurance this gave parents cut down on the number of false alarms I had to cope with.

When our school system was centralized in 1951, with new elementary schools built in Cleveland and Constantia and a new high school built in Central Square, I moved my immunization clinics to these buildings. I continued to give all the shots myself, with the help of the school nurses, except at the high school, where I was assisted by Dr. Edward Murphy, health officer for the town of Hastings. Our results were very good, giving protection to between seventy and eighty percent of all the school children and preschoolers in the area.

It wasn't until the early seventies, when the County Health Department took over the immunization clinics, that a hugh drop-off occurred in the number of school children receiving protective shots. Once the clinics were no longer held in the schools, fewer children were immunized, since the only clinic held in our area by the county health department was conducted monthly in West Monroe, about ten miles from Cleveland.

After about four years of this, I pleaded with the Oswego County Health Department to allow us—the remaining local

119

health officers—to conduct our clinics as we had done before the health department took charge. I asked only that it provide the vaccines, syringes, needles, and other materials we needed. The health department agreed and even donated the services of its nurses. So I returned to the school immunization business, hoping to regain the high level of protection against communicable disease we had achieved in earlier years. Nationwide, immunization clinics such as those I conducted have all but conquered most communicable diseases; diphtheria, tetanus, polio, smallpox, and whooping cough have almost disappeared, and even mumps, rubella, and rubeola are not the dreads of childhood they once were.

Medicine has changed in many ways other than those I have discussed here. The house calls and home deliveries that were routine in my early years of practice have become rarities (although, as I stated in the Foreword, they seem to be making a comeback). The status of general practice as a whole has undergone some ups and downs over my career, too. After World War II, great changes began to take place in American medicine, one of which was the organization of general practitioners into county, state, and national bodies of strength. I joined this movement at all three levels in the late 1940s. Dr. William Buecheler was an early leader of these movements in the Syracuse area. After the American Academy of General Practice was founded in 1947, Dr. Buecheler persuaded many of us generalists in Central New York to join it along with him. Thus I became a member of this academy in 1949 and have maintained my membership ever since.

In October 1949, the Onondaga County affiliate hosted the first state convention in Syracuse. I served on the convention committee and took charge of the scientific, educational, and pharmaceutical booths, while Bee co-chaired the hospitality committee.

For a time during the 1950s and 1960s, however, the rise of the medical specialist threatened to swamp the field of general

ADVANCES AND CHANGES

practice altogether. Specialists argued that it was hard enough to keep up with medical developments in a small area of expertise; the G.P. couldn't hope to remain informed of the sweeping changes occuring in medicine as a whole. Certainly, keeping abreast of developments was a difficult task for the G.P., but it was far from impossible. The practice of medicine is a continual learning experience, and I, like other G.P.'s, became adept at learning from a myriad of sources.

As I have mentioned before, the surgical locker-rooms and the cloakrooms of our hospitals serve as fine classrooms for learning from our peers—those physicians we encounter in our daily rounds—and hospital staff meetings can be another fruitful source of education. Representatives of drug companies and manufacturers of medical equipment, who often crowd our offices to sell their products, are another source of information, providing a multitude of detail in person and in the literature they leave behind. Then there are the medical magazines—it seems as if hundreds of them fill the mailbox daily. During my medical career I always seemed to be reading a medical article in my spare time, neglecting other types of reading material altogether. The various medical conventions and meetings I have attended over the years also contributed to my ongoing education. And finally, of course, there are always formal medical courses offered to help keep the doctor up with the newest advances in medications, surgery, and the rest of the specialties.

The dedicated physician, including the G.P., takes advantage of all these avenues of medical learning. I learned early in my practice to avail myself of them. I believed that as a G.P. I should be sufficiently informed to recognize what kind of medical attention my patients needed and to ensure that, if I couldn't provide it myself, I could at least seek referrals for them to men of caliber in the appropriate specialties.

Among the formal courses I took over the years, I remember especially a two-week course in electrocardiography that I attended at the Mount Sinai Hospital in New York City in 1951.

The course was directed by Dr. Arthur Masters, one of the leading cardiologists of the day. It taught me basic EKG interpretation and gave me a great background for other cardiology courses that I took later. It was an interesting two weeks. Several physicians from the Syracuse area were attending the course too, and we would all lunch together. We engaged a taxi to meet us at the hospital entrance every noon and drive us to the famous Lindy's Restaurant on Times Square. There we would discuss the morning session while filling up on sandwiches topped off with a generous portion of cherry or strawberry cheesecake—just what doctors studying heart medicine should be eating, of course!

On Thursdays for several years afterward, I took courses in various aspects of medicine offered by the Department of Medicine of the Upstate Medical Center of Syracuse. These courses varied in length from one week to seven weeks, and certificates were given for some of them. After a seven-week course on School Health in 1958, my status in the American School Health Association was raised from regular membership to Fellowship, and I remained a Fellow until my retirement.

The ongoing education I engaged in was common to G.P.s of my day. But the belief that G.P.s were somehow less educated than the other doctors because they pursued breadth rather than depth of knowledge continued to undermine the field; and for a time it seemed that G.P.s were an endangered species.

Many organizations continued to challenge this misconception and to fight for recognition of the worth of general practice. In February 1965, I was given an opportunity to take a hand in this battle. At the annual meeting of the New York State Medical Society, I was elected chairman of the section on General Practice, a job that entailed setting up a program for the Society's 1966 meeting. At that time, the teaching of general practice in medical schools was still frowned upon, but, given the headway being made at the time by the American Academy of General Practice, I decided to give the issue an airing. As the subject of my symposium, therefore, I chose the delicate and controversial question, "Shall General Practice Departments be Established in our Medical Schools?"

Dr. Harrel, the Dean of the Hershey Medical School, and Dr. Nicholas Pisacano, who later became the executive secretary of the American Board of Family Practice, spoke in favor of such departments, while the deans of two medical schools in New York City vigorously opposed them. When the floor was opened for general questions, I had difficulty as the moderator recognizing the speakers amid the din. So heated was the discussion that nearly all those present were shouting at once!

At the end of the session, no conclusion had been reached, but I was satisfied nevertheless; at least the issue had been brought into the open. Soon afterward, New York State's legislative body, and those of other states, mandated the teaching of general practice in their medical schools. Today, departments of family practice are common in most teaching hospitals across the country.

By 1971, the battle to prove the worth of the G.P. seemed nearly won. The American Academy of General Practice changed its name to the American Academy of Family Physicians, heralding the rebirth of general practice in the new guise of family practice. To combat the belief that family practitioners were less educated than other doctors, it became the first medical organization to require yearly post-graduate study in order to maintain membership; compliance was checked every three years. I met the requirements regularly until my retirement in 1982, when I was given a life membership.

Another change that has taken place in medicine since I began to practice is the astronomical rise in its cost. Some of this rise may be due to the many technological advances for diagnosis and treatment that have developed over the same period. However, much of the rise in costs can be attributed to the concurrent rise in malpractice cases in recent years.

Malpractice is defined in Funk and Wagnal's dictionary as "the improper, injurious, or negligent treatment of a patient."

HOUSE CALLS

The increasing number of lawsuits charging malpractice is also forcing up the costs of medical care. As more and more malpractice lawsuits are tried in court, jury damage awards of $1 million and up are becoming commonplace; thus, doctors must pay increasing insurance premiums in order to continue to practice medicine. In the early fifties, my premium was between $500 and $600 a year; when I last checked, this figure had risen to between $8,000 and $9,000. For neurosurgeons it is now between $40,000 and $50,000. And these spiraling costs, increasing yearly, are passed on to the patient.

In cases of genuine malpractice, awards should be made. But many lawsuits have to do with unhappy results rather than doctors' mistakes: maloccurance rather than malpractice. Our patients expect that the great advances that have been made in medicine should give them perfect results; when that doesn't happen, many sue. One result is higher medical costs for all; another may be poorer medical care. Only when you talk to a doctor who has been sued for malpractice can you understand the demoralizing effect it can have on him—and on his work.

In a 1984 report by the A.M.A., "Professional Liability in the '80s," a study was made of the effects of malpractice suits on doctors' professional efficiency. A random sample of 154 doctors sued for malpractice in Cook County, Illinois, was surveyed. Most experienced anger, and twenty-five physicians—18.8 percent—said they felt a "loss of nerve in some clinical situations." Twenty-eight percent stopped performing certain high-risk procedures, and 42 percent stopped seeing certain kinds of patients. Fourteen percent said their medical practices had suffered, and one third of the sample group—33.6 percent—thought about early retirement after being sued. Just over one third—39 percent—admitted to four or five symptoms suggestive of severe depression after the malpractice suit, and 8 percent fell ill during the litigation. All these results occurred despite the fact that 75 percent of doctors who went on trial for malpractice in Cook County won their cases. The researchers

ADVANCES AND CHANGES

concluded that such effects could adversely affect the delivery of health care.

Increasing litigation and rising medical costs are worrisome changes affecting the practice of medicine. But overall, the changes that have occurred over my career have been good ones. Not only has medicine become better and faster at saving lives, it has become better at making those lives safe, comfortable, and worth living.

Nine
A Sister and a Daughter

The war was over, and the forties passed quickly and busily for our family; the fifties promised to be no less hectic—and no less interesting. Our boys were growing up fast, and as concerned parents, Bee and I took on many jobs that we hoped would improve our community and, thus, our sons' lives.

I had been a member of the local school board in the early 1940s, so I had been in on the centralization of the local school system, which began to go into effect in 1951. It was a big, complex job since parts of three counties were involved. Bee, however, saw in this change an extra opportunity for the children of Cleveland. With centralization, the old Union Free School in Cleveland was to be abandoned. The school was an old, boxy, wooden building standing in about ten acres of land, right in the center of the village. The Cleveland Village Board had advertised the property, hoping to interest a small business or factory in locating there, but nothing came of this idea. Bee, however, had a plan of her own. She decided that the site would make a perfect public playground for the children of Cleveland.

She investigated and found that if the local community raised $500 to create or maintain such a playground, the state would match that amount. But where could she drum up $500?

Bee first tried the village board, the owners of the property, but many old timers were against the idea and certainly weren't willing to invest in it. She did persuade the board to lease her the property for $1, providing it was used only for recreational purposes for the village children. The board agreed to this, sure that Bee would fail to raise the money she needed and that the scheme would come to nothing.

First, she paid $20 of her own money to have a title search made and then leased the property from the village for $1. Then she formed a committee with several other leading citizens of Cleveland and marched door to door with the other members, soliciting funds. Bee could be very persuasive; the supporters and dollars for the playground grew steadily in number. By late 1951, Bee and the committee had collected the entire amount and been promised a matching $500 from New York State. The playground was no longer a pipedream.

The following spring, Bee hired William Hoeppel of Central Square to supervise the new playground for the summer at a weekly salary of $50. She enlisted our three older boys and many other village children to clean up the grounds around the old schoolhouse. After the final session of school was held in the building that June, Bee and a troupe of other volunteers, both adults and children, cleaned and scrubbed the entire inside of the building. Finally both school and grounds were ready. The playground was open.

The first few days of operation, children came but seemed rather subdued. Soon, though, Bill Hoeppel's lively personality broke the ice and children were drawn to the new playground for games, story readings, and other planned activities. On rainy days, the clean schoolhouse came alive again as children gathered there for indoor games, debates, record playing, and dancing. The summer flew by, and families with children became enthusiastic about the new playground.

For two more years, Bee and her committee had to beg for dollars to keep the playground going, but then their hard work paid off. Arthur Lawson, the village mayor, lived across the street from the playground. He had watched the children gravitate there for three years in a row; he had seen them playing and learning in a safe, supervised environment. By the end of the third summer, he had changed his mind about Bee's crazy scheme. He talked the village board into taking back the property and running the playground itself. Today Bee's playground is still going strong; on summer evenings, it often seems as if half of Cleveland is gathered there, the children working off their energy in softball games, the adults watching and talking with their neighbors.

The playground was far from being Bee's only preoccupation during the early fifties. Soon after the new Cleveland elementary school opened, Bee organized a mothers' club, and, later, the P.T.O. and P.T.A. groups. Moreover, now that our fourth son, Stephen, was in school, our house was empty of children during the day, giving Bee yet more time for her various causes. As the doctor's wife in a small community, Bee was, like it or not, a leading citizen and was asked to head many charitable drives in the area. Fortunately, Bee was a great organizer, and had fun carrying out these tasks. Over the years, she headed fundraising drives for cancer research, heart research, TB research, and the March of Dimes. She did such a good job that later on she became a board member of the Oswego County TB, RD, and Heart Associations, and of the New York State TB and RD Associations, and, finally, the president of the Oswego County Health Association, which she reorganized almost singlehandedly. I remember once, accompanying Bee to New York City for a state RD association meeting, being identified as "Bee Brown's husband." I was taken aback for a moment, but then beamed with pride at my wife's accomplishments.

While Bee was working to improve the community, she was also running the house, chauffeuring the boys and their friends, and keeping me happy. Her endurance was a constant source of wonder to me. By seven in the morning, she was up and working: getting breakfast, getting the boys off to school, cleaning the house, answering the telephone (no small task in a doctor's household, where often she had to calm anxious patients before even finding out what was wrong, or reel off, yet again, the ingredients for a baby formula to a new mother), helping me in the office, getting supper, putting the boys to bed, and then often staying up until 1:00 in the morning ironing the boys' shirts and other clothes needed for the next day. The late-night hours were often the only chance Bee and I had to see each other in peace; many a night I would stay up to talk with her or watch some of the new late-night television shows with her while the ironrite took in the clothes Bee fed it.

Meanwhile, our boys were growing fast. In 1951, the time came for Neal's Bar Mitzvah, the first in our family. In the Jewish religion, the Bar Mitzvah celebrates a boy's religious coming of age, and the Bat Mitzvah celebrates a girl's. At that time, however, children in our religious school were encouraged to complete their religious education and receive confirmation certificates in a ceremony coinciding with the spring holiday of Shavuoth; often, therefore, parents didn't think it necessary for their children to undergo the additional instruction needed to prepare them for a Bar Mitzvah or Bat Mitzvah. We did, however, and arranged for Neal's Bar Mitzvah to take place in September. An old friend of mine from Syracuse, Rabbi Jesse Ross, prepared our son for the ceremony, and Neal performed beautifully. He read from the Torah in Hebrew without a single error, and Bee and I swelled with pride at our thirteen-year-old son's style. The sanctuary of our temple was filled with well-wishers that morning, most of them having come all the way from Cleveland to celebrate the day with us in Syracuse. When the ceremony was over, the speeches made, and the gifts given, I remember thinking, "Well, that's one launched. Will my other three measure up?"

Over the years, of course, they measured up beautifully. Miner's Bar Mitzvah took place two years later; Terry's, three years after that; and Stephen's four years after Terry's.

Neal's Bar Mitzvah officially marked his religious coming

A SISTER AND A DAUGHTER

of age, but many other experiences also shaped his future. One rather unfortunate episode occurred in 1953, when he was fifteeen.

Just as Bee was asked to live up to her role of "doctor's wife," so community expectations affected my sons. One Thursday, when Bee and I were away on our weekly outing, the local ambulance crew came to the house to find me. A young boy from the village had been accidentally shot in the chest with a shotgun and needed emergency aid. This was in the early days of our ambulance service, and the volunteer drivers and attendants had no first aid skills; they responded quickly and took the patients to the hospital as speedily as possible, and that was all. Dismayed to find me gone, the ambulance crew decided that Neal, as the doctor's son, was the next best person to care for the shooting victim on the trip to the hospital. They asked Neal to sit in the ambulance with the boy and hold a compress dressing on his awful wound on the twenty-mile trip to Oneida.

Neal rose to the occasion and did as they asked, but to his dismay and grief, the boy died. The episode made a lasting negative impression on my son, helping to steer him away from all thoughts of a career in medicine. As the saying goes, "Doctors' sons become lawyers, and lawyers' sons, doctors." In time, Neal did become a lawyer.

As our sons grew up and began following their own paths in life, Bee and I almost gave up hope of ever having a daughter, something all six of us had wanted for years. But in 1953, a girl came into our lives in a most unexpected way.

Our introduction to Gerda came about by sheer luck in April 1953. Bee was in Syracuse, waiting for the boys to get out of their religious education classes, when she got a telephone call. It was from Mrs. George Goldstein, the Central New York Chairman of the American Field Service. She wanted Bee to stop by her house and learn about the A.F.S.

Bee knew nothing of this organization, but she soon learned,

131

and so did we. Originally formed by American students in Europe who volunteered to drive ambulances for the French army during World War I before the U.S. entered the war, the A.F.S. kept a loose organization going after the war ended. Then its director, Stephen Gallati, reactivated the organization during World War II. When that war ended, its directors decided that its ideal—an open door to understanding and friendship among the peoples of the world—might best be served by a program which would bring European teenage students to the United States for a year of study. The first group of fifty students arrived in the U.S. in 1947; since then, the program has grown and prospered and now also allows American teenagers to go to countries in Europe and other continents throughout the globe.

Mrs. Goldstein explained the goals of the A.F.S. to Bee and the boys and asked if our family would be interested in accepting a foreign student for a year. With an open mind, but mixed feelings, Bee said she would like to consider the responsibility and talk it over with the whole family before coming to a decision. Mrs. Goldstein agreed and gave Bee the dossiers of two foreign students as possible guests, a German boy and a Viennese girl. "The girl has to be placed in a Jewish home," said Mrs. Goldstein casually. "But of course, you don't have to accept either student."

Bee and I talked the idea over, alone and with the boys. We decided that the experience might be interesting for all of us. Once we had decided to take part in the A.F.S., it took us no time at all to decide which student to take: The family voted unanimously for the girl. The boys had always wanted a sister. Moreover, the girl had been attending a boy's gymnasium (high school) in Vienna, so she was used to boys. Also, she was of our own faith.

Bee told Mrs. Goldstein of our decision, and the process was set in motion: sailing times, bus schedules, visas—it seemed that it would be a long time before we would get to meet this Gerda Brandl. In June, once everything was set, we had a picture taken of our whole family, and Bee enclosed it, with a long letter, to the Brandl family. She described the way we lived, our school system, and reassured the Brandls that we were Jewish—their one stipulation about a family. In early July, we got two letters in return, one from Gerda and one from her mother. Both put us in a high state of excitement.

Mrs. Brandl's letter touched Bee and me deeply. "Gerda is our only child," she wrote, "and we are extremely fond of her, and it might be that the crucial years we spent with her in the emigration made us feel more attached to each other than it is in other families. In making the application for Gerda we realized that a scholarship would be the chance of her life; however, the idea of being a full year without her seemed very hard to me. We are extremely happy to find in your letter this wonderful spirit of a happy family. . . . I am perfectly sure that you will find Gerda an ever gay and agreeable house companion who will easily adapt herself to your family life.

"We too are faithful to the creed of our ancestors and it means a lot for me and my husband that there will be no conflict of conscience. . . . We suffered a lot from Nazi despotism and for nearly eight years we were in emigration, whereby several years were spent in an Hungarian concentration camp. Almost all members of my numerous family were killed and Dr. Brandl lost two relatives. In 1945 we returned to Vienna where my husband tried very hard to rebuild and establish a new life for us. . . . We have been looking forward to Gerda's departure with mixed feelings but your dear letter gave us the relief we wanted. Now we will be perfectly at ease when she will leave us. . . . I am yours very thankfully. /S/Lilly Brandl."

"Kindly tell me if winter time is very severe? Do you want me to give her snowboots and woolen underwear? With kindest regards, /S/D. Ernst Brandl."

Gerda's letter had a different flavor—effervescent and, as her mother put it, "ever gay."

"Dear Mrs. Brown, Mr. Brown, and my dear little brothers:

HOUSE CALLS

I want to explain to you my great happiness, which I felt, when I received your dear letter a few days ago. I confess, that all the time, since I know about my opportunity to study one year in the U.S.A., I had been somehow afraid to be so far from my parents in a foreign country and with quite strange people, but now, since I have your photo and your letter in my hands, I feel, if I would know you all since my earliest childhood. So I'll be able to leave my parents even for one year with a glad heart, and I'm sure they don't need to be anxious for me. As I am the only child at home, I'm looking forward to have soon your so nice brothers. Is Steve going to school already?

"In Austria, school is over since July 4, and now I enjoy the holidays very much. I am very fond of swimming and of trips. I like tennis very much too, but I play only since last year, so that I am not the best player. I've heard so much about baseball; but in Austria nobody plays this game and so I'm looking forward to become acquainted with this and surely other new games too.

"In Austria there are eight grades in a high school. I'm going in the sixth and would come there continuous to the seventh. So that summer 1955 I shall be able to graduate and go to college (University). But as you wrote me, I have the chance to come in U.S. to the graduating class already. As I've heard schooling is not so difficult in U.S. as in Austria and therefore I would be very happy to be able to graduate in U.S.A. At school I'm learning English, Latin, Greek (Ancient Greek) and beside school French and Hebrew. I would be very thankful, if I would be able to learn Latin and French in Cleveland at school. But I don't know, do American students learn Latin and Greek too?

"Is the high school Neal attends in Cleveland or in Syracuse? I'm very happy, that I may go with him to the same school, there is much more fun, if two of the same family attend the same school. Are there many exercises at school? In Austria we have to learn almost all the day long.

A SISTER AND A DAUGHTER

"As my mother is not quite healthy, I help her often in the kitchen and so I would like to help you too. . . . Yours very, very thankfully, /S/ Gerda Brandl."

After these letters, the waiting period seemed even harder to bear. But finally, the day of her arrival came: August 19, 1953. The bus carrying the Central New York A.S.F.ers was due in Syracuse at about 5:00 P.M. So as not to overwhelm Gerda, Bee and I left the boys in Cleveland and drove to Syracuse by ourselves to meet her.

Naturally, the bus was two hours late. We talked with other host parents also waiting, and strained our eyes watching for the bus. Finally it pulled in. For several minutes all was turmoil and confusion, but then a dark-haired girl separated herself from the crowd: It was Gerda.

We were thrilled to see her. She met all our expectations. Of medium build, she had a fair complexion and clear hazel eyes. We immediately seemed to understand each other. It was the beginning of a lifelong relationship. We had our daughter at last.

Gerda's meeting with the boys was equally successful. Miner was away at camp, but Gerda's greetings with Neal, Terry, and Stephen were warm and excited. A flood of talk carried us upstairs to the guest room we had prepared for her, and then back downstairs for supper.

The next few days were confusing but exciting for us all. Everything seemed new and different to Gerda, but she adapted quickly and soon became a part of our family, as if, indeed, she had known us since her "earliest childhood." Her warmth, vivacity, and charm captivated us all.

I will always recall dinnertimes of that year. I generally managed to have dinner with my family, and the extra place set for Gerda that year gave me a sense of pride. Gerda would help Bee in the kitchen, preparing the food, setting the table, and cleaning up afterward. Always the pair of them were talking and laughing. At the table, the conversation bristled with tales of school and teenage affairs and with Gerda's continual questions, always preceeded with "Mommie " or "Daddy."

Gerda's visit was not without its rough spots, however. A high-spirited girl cannot hold her own with four boys without some argument. Time after time I had to go upstairs to settle family fights that had been brought to my attention by loud noises and the patter of running feet. Only in later years did I find out how wrong I was to put the blame most of the time on the boys! But the arguments were like all arguments within families; they were fought on the surface, above a strong undercurrent of love and respect. Bee and I often relived that year in our memories.

Gerda settled right in at school too. As the first A.F.S. student in our school system, she set a role model that was difficult to beat. She held her own scholastically and soon became friends with her classmates. Her teachers, too, seemed to like her fresh approach and her enthusiasm.

True to our promise to her parents, we made sure that Gerda was able to go to synagogue regularly. In September, we took her to our synagogue for the high holy days services. Because her stricter religious upbringing didn't allow her to ride in a car on those days, she stayed the night in Syracuse with Bee's parents—her "American grandparents," as she called them.

We also introduced Gerda to the children of some of our Syracuse friends so that she could make friends with people other than her classmates. And we took part with Gerda in several A.F.S. gatherings, where students from many nations would perform in their native dress, singing and dancing. Gerda formed friendships with many of her peers; some of those friendships have lasted to this day.

Gerda's Syracuse friendships led to our only serious confrontation with her. At first, she felt somewhat closer to these Syracuse girls than to her Central Square classmates and decided that she would like to attend their high school in Syracuse while continuing to live with us. Discussion about the difficulties this would involve failed to change her mind; she was determined. It took consultations with Mrs. Goldstein and the New York A.F.S. office to persuade her to abandon this idea. It was clear that this Austrian girl had a mind of her own and liked to have things done her way.

Over her year with us, however, we slowly learned of the crucible that had formed this strong will: the war.

Although the Nazis occupied Austria early in 1938, it wasn't until March of that year, when the Nazis took over Austria, that Gerda's father, a physician, was forced to leave his home and practice in the town of Mattasburg, sixty kilometers from Vienna. Ernst was ordered out of his office, his home was taken from him, and he and the other Jews of Mattasburg were commanded to leave. Before being allowed to go, however, they were humiliated by the Nazi conquerors—forced to get down on their hands and knees and clean the cobblestones of the main street with toothbrushes.

Ernst, his wife Lilly, and Gerda, then two and a half years old, grabbed what they could carry and set out from their home, hoping to reach relatives in Budapest. Ernst and Lilly knew that the Nazis could change their minds at any time and turn a sentence of exile into a sentence of death. So the little family traveled only at night, hiding out during the day wherever they could. In this way—on foot and by night, hampered by a two-year-old child—the Brandls covered over 200 kilometers. Once, Nazi soldiers were so close that Lilly had to gag Gerda to prevent the little girl from crying out.

Miraculously, the family did reach Budapest. There, Ernst and Lilly left Gerda with relatives while they hid out in attics and basements belonging to relatives and, later, to non-Jewish friends. Ernst was finally able to get forged papers; with them, he procured a job as a doctor in an International Red Cross Camp on the outskirts of Budapest. He went there daily and was able to sneak out food for his wife and friends.

It was four years before the family was reunited. Ernst and

Lilly had been living in a displaced persons' camp, but finally they managed to rent a one-room apartment in Budapest and bring their daughter home. The family lived in these cramped, but comparatively blissful, conditions for one year, until finally they were allowed to return to their home in Austria.

Their homecoming was grim, however. They found that fifty-seven members of their families had been killed in the Nazi gas chambers. Dr. Brandl was so shaken and disillusioned by these experiences that he was unable to return to medical practice. Instead, the Brandls moved to Vienna, where Ernst opened a dry goods store—one of his family's businesses—in an attempt to make a living. It was hard going at first, but he was able to keep his little family alive—and together.

With such a childhood behind her, it was no wonder that Gerda had a strong will; the miracle was that she was so vivacious and warm-hearted.

As her months with us passed, Gerda grew ever closer to our family; soon we were making plans for Neal to make a summer visit to her home as an A.F.S. student. Meanwhile, both Gerda and Neal were preparing to graduate from high school. Soon it was time for the senior prom, and Gerda, invited by a fellow fraternity member of Neal's, took the occasion very seriously. She decided to wear a pair of high-heeled shoes, which we had recently given her on her birthday, to the dance, so for days before the prom we would hear her thumping up and down the upstairs hallway in an attempt to break them in and to keep her balance at the same time. I don't know whether the shoes were comfortable, but Gerda certainly seemed to have a good time.

On June 21, Neal left with seventy-four other A.F.S. "ambassadors" for Europe, and on June 29, Gerda received her high school diploma from the Central Square High School. It was a proud day for the Browns—not only Gerda but Neal, in absentia, graduated that day. But it was also a sad day; we knew Gerda's visit was almost over. On August 16, armed with two of her new loves, corn flakes and ketchup, Gerda boarded the bus in Syracuse on the first leg of her journey back to Austria. The whole family (except for Neal, already in Austria) came to see her off, and it was a sad and tearful occasion. Of course, Bee and Gerda were the biggest crybabies of all. Once the bus was out of sight, we got back in our car and drove the thirty miles to Cleveland in almost perfect silence, all of us deep in our own thoughts.

Gerda soon proved that she was truly a daughter and a sister to the Browns, however; she called us that first night and wrote us many times even before she left the United States. And since that first trip, she has visited us many times and written to us regularly, in a style as lively and charming as she is herself. Through her letters and visits, we participated in her triumphs, her loves, and tragedies: her parents' deaths, her engagement and marriage, the births of her children. We can never be sufficiently grateful for the chance that led Mrs. Goldstein to hand Gerda's dossier to Bee.

With Gerda gone for the time being, Bee's and my thoughts turned to the next big hurdle: getting Neal off to college. A year earlier, we had picked the school he was to go to: Hamilton College in Clinton, New York, less than an hour's drive from Cleveland. Neal and I had driven there and looked the campus and facilities over, and, the spring before he graduated from high school, he received a letter accepting his application.

Neal's trip to Austria had cut into his orientation week at Hamilton College, so Bee and I met him in New York City and drove him directly there. We had a surprise for him, however. A week earlier, Bee and I had driven to Hamilton College and arranged Neal's room in his dorm, cleaning it, putting up curtains, and making it as homelike as possible. It was an attempt to make his transition to life at college as easy as possible, and he seemed to like it. We got him settled in and left. It seemed as if our children were all leaving at once!

Neal seemed to fit in well at Hamilton, which made his

absence easier to bear. His course work in his pre-law curriculum kept him busy, and before long he had made many friends, soon joining a fraternity. On Parents' Day, in April 1955, Bee and I drove there to see Neal and meet his fraternity brothers and their families and dates. Neal and I were talking in the main living room of the fraternity house when suddenly we heard music, laughter, and clapping coming from the room below. "I bet that's mother," Neal exclaimed, and we went to investigate. Sure enough, as we hurried downstairs we could see Bee doing the Charleston in center stage to the cheers and applause of her audience. Neal was embarrassed at first, but soon he was receiving congratulations on his mother's great style in dancing. As for me, I was used to it.

With Gerda gone and Neal at college, our lives in Cleveland settled down into their usual half-frantic state: School activities, dance revues, Boy Scout outings, summer camps, graduations, confirmation services, and Bar Mitzvahs—often in conflict—kept us on the go whenever we weren't working. It was life as usual once again!

Ten
Labors of Love

A country doctor has a special place in his community. His neighbors and patients look to him for more than just medical care. Because of this, he often has responsibilities outside those directly related to his practice urged on him by the community; I was no exception. Over my years in Cleveland, I acted at various times as health officer for three townships, coroner's physician, school physician, and camp doctor for four summer camps. I have already described the duties involved in the posts of coroner's physician and camp doctor and in the immunization clinics I ran as school physician. My post as school doctor entailed other duties as well.

In the 1940s, the job included conducting physical examinations for the students of several schools in the area, in both Oswego and Oneida Counties. With Bee acting as my aide during the early years, I would visit many one-room schools and examine each child. I checked for tonsillar enlargements, glandular defects, dental caries, ear diseases, heart mumurs, abnormal chest sounds, herniae, undescended testes, and abnormal growth patterns. For these exams I was paid the princely sum of 50¢ per student. Many times performing these physicals was difficult and embarrasing, because, for lack of a better place, they took place in front of the class at the teacher's desk, with the teacher holding up a sheet to provide some privacy.

After the school system was centralized in the early 1950s, I was hired as the chief school physician for the new Central Square Central School District, a post I retained until my retirement. Olive Getman, a young woman from Constantia, soon became the district's head nurse, and, with the help of the rest of the medical staff, we soon set up a secondary school medical organization which I can boast was second to none.

We did regular school physical examinations and routine tuberculosis skin testing, and we gave each student a screening urinalysis at least once a year. We had an immunization record of more than 75 percent. We took care of in-school emergencies and routinely checked the safety precautions of the various school buildings. I did most of the athletic physical examinations—and managed to be present at most of the home football games! We gave service when and where it was needed without question or hesitation, and not once in all the years I served in this post were any of the staff criticized for neglect of duty.

The job was not without its tricky side, however. It takes more than medical skill to examine skittish adolescents or frightened children. One thing I was supposed to check for was lumps in the breasts of adolescent girls. Since actually touching their breasts was out of the question, I attempted to fulfill this requirement by simply looking for any visible lumps and asking the girls if they had noticed any. Once, however, even this delicate approach failed to save me from reproach. At that time, Bee was serving on the school board. A fellow member came up and told her that the board had received a complaint about me; a girl I had examined had asserted that I had "visually raped" her. Quick as a flash, Bee responded, "Well, I knew Marv was good, but I didn't know he was that good!"

The job also had its grim moments. There were many poor people in the school district who, even with the best will in the world, couldn't adequately provide for their children. All too often, I would examine children who were underfed or underclothed for the weather. Many times when I found children in need, I would send them to our home for a little tender loving care from Bee. On the cold days of winter she would often feed their skinny bodies and put warm socks or stockings on their bare feet and legs, swollen and purple from exposure. I remember one bitter day in January 1946 when I was called by Anne Welch, then the principal of the old Union School in Cleveland, to attend to a six-year-old girl named Marjorie who had frostbitten legs and feet. She had walked a mile to school on this sub-zero morning wearing only sandals without stockings, a light dress, and a worn-out, threadbare coat, with no covering for her head. After examining and treating her, I brought her home. Bee gradually warmed her up from the inside out with hot cocoa and cereal, rubbed her limbs to improve her circulation, and dressed her in some of our boys' warm clothes. The only residual effects were some blisters that I continued to treat for a few days after she'd returned to her thankless parents.

There were times when I encountered children suffering from more than the unintentional neglect that comes from poverty. In the early 1960s, I was called to attend a young boy of eight, after his teacher had noticed many black and blue marks on his body. When I examined him at the new Cleveland Elementary School, I found many bad bruises and a number of old scars. He broke down and told me that his father was in the habit of beating him and his siblings to discipline them.

I reported his case to the child welfare authorities, and charges were brought against the boy's father. In Children's Court, the father admitted to the beatings, stating that it was his right as a parent to teach his children right from wrong, and that beating his children was his way of doing it. The judge gave the man a suspended sentence for child abuse and told him that any further beatings of his children would send him to jail. Evidently the threat worked; no more bruises were found.

HOUSE CALLS

One of the biggest tasks I took on over my career was my work as health officer. From the time I began my practice on September 1, 1938, until the health district was abolished on December 19, 1971, I acted as health officer for the Consolidated Health District of the Town of Constantia, which included the Village of Cleveland. After 1971, the Oswego County Health Department took over and retained my services as the deputy health officer for the Town of Constantia.

In March 1944, I was also appointed health officer for the Town of Vienna, which is in Oneida County, east of Cleveland, and included the village of Sylvan Beach, and in the fifties I became health officer for the Town of West Monroe, west of Cleveland. So, at one point, my jurisdiction as health officer extended from the outlet of Oneida Lake all the way north and west; east along State Route 49 to Herter's Bridge and the Town of Rome, and west to the western edge of the Town of West Monroe, almost to Brewerton, along the northern fringes of Oneida Lake.

This was a huge area, and the tasks it entailed were many. Since I served longest and was most closely concerned with the Town of Constantia, however, I will concentrate my description of the job of health officer on that area.

The three most important goals I set myself as health officer for the Town of Constantia were (1) a clean and sanitary milk supply through pasteurization of all milk distributed in my jurisdiction; (2) a clean and sanitary water supply for the area; and (3) the establishment of a proper sewage disposal system.

I began with high hopes and plenty of energy and determination, and in the end they paid off, but I soon learned that the wheels of government—at the local level as much as at the national level—grind slowly. Even at the level of the health board of a single township, politics are apt to skip into any discussion, complicating decisions on all issues and making progress agonizingly slow. Nevertheless, progress was made.

When I arrived in Cleveland, there were about twelve one-cow dairies and at least two farms that had milk routes in the Town of Constantia. Besides the two regular milk deliveries, all these dealers were producing, distributing, and selling raw milk in containers brought to them by their customers; I was determined to bring this state of affairs to an end.

This first objective didn't take too long to achieve. At my urging, the local board of health passed a resolution in December 1938 that only Grade A pasteurized milk could be sold in the Town of Constantia. The milk dealers were given until March 1, 1939, to comply.

My second goal—a clean and sanitary water supply—took almost thirteen years to accomplish. The local water supply came from natural springs north of Cleveland; this spring water was routed by sluiceways into a large reservoir built just north of the village in the early part of the century. The water was clear (most of the time), tasty, and soft—but the supply was often contaminated by colon bacilli that found their way into the reservoir from animal droppings. Furthermore, the water often became murky from soil erosion after a rain or in the spring when melting snow would wash soil into the reservoir.

The common treatment for purifying the water was chlorination—but it took me years to convince the local health board to agree to the process. Throughout the 1940s, I pleaded and argued and reasoned in vain; the local health board, led by Harry Best, then Cleveland's mayor, was suspicious of chlorination and reluctant to spend the money needed to initiate it. I brought the issue up year after year with no success. Finally, however, I turned the trick in 1951 by means of a ruse. For two days in May of that year, I treated many residents of Cleveland for gastro-enteritis. It seemed that the telephone was ringing constantly as patients called for help, all complaining of the same symptoms, though in varying degrees of severity: nausea, vomiting, abdominal cramps, diarrhea, fever, and weakness.

"Finally," I thought, "Here is the evidence I need to convince the board of health that our water supply must be made potable and safe." In fact, I had no scientific evidence that the epidemic was caused by drinking water. I did not have the water tested. My evidence was clinical only.

Nevertheless, it convinced Dr. Walter Levy, the District State Health Officer in Syracuse. I wrote him a letter saying that an outbreak of gastro-enteritis affected sixty to seventy percent of the residents of Cleveland, and that since there was no other common source of infection, such as milk or other food, I believed the cause of the illness was the drinking water. He agreed and wrote in June to my board of health, strongly urging that the water supply of the Village of Cleveland be chlorinated. "From our previous knowledge of the bacteriological examination of the water supply of the Village of Cleveland," he wrote, "we know that this water supply is subject to pollution. I believe that your conclusion that this outbreak was water-borne is amply justified by the evidence you present. At this time, I strongly urge that the Board of Trustees of the village arrange to protect the water supply of the village by the installation of chlorination equipment."

I read this letter to the board, and a heated discussion followed. Harry Best still would not give in. He thought that a high fence built around the reservoir would keep the contamination under control. Finally, however, another member made a motion that the board of health go on record as favoring chlorination and recommending that the Water Board proceed with the installation of such a system.

The motion was seconded and passed—a great step forward. Even this, however, did not result in action for more than four months. Then, Dr. Herman Hilleboe, the New York State Commissioner of Health (urged by Dr. Levy), ordered the water board to chlorinate the water supply forthwith. And even after the process began, it wasn't until September 1953—nearly two years later—that the chlorination plant finally became operational.

Even this snail's pace beat that at which progress was made toward my third goal—establishing a proper sewage disposal system. I did not achieve it before my retirement, and although steps have been made in the right direction, it looks as if such a system won't be set up before the end of this decade.

Other important goals were accomplished, however. A town dump was set up, and widespread immunization against communicable diseases was achieved, for example.

In the sixties, a new issue began to surface in my area: pollution in Oneida Lake. The sixties was a decade of increasing awareness of environmental issues generally, and increasing algae growth in Oneida Lake brought the problem to the fore.

Being a eutrophic lake (one with a reduced level of dissolved oxygen, thus favoring plant life over animal life) with a large water shed and sufficient outlets, Oneida Lake was never tagged as truly polluted; its fish remained edible and its waters clean enough to swim in. An overgrowth of algae and the presence of a green-blue scum covering its surface during the summer months led many people to complain about pollution, however. Moreover, in many small bays, the algae would trap dead fish and fecal material, causing a noticeable smell. This nuisance was easily correctable, however; the landowners in these bay areas simply had to cut down the algae trapping these materials.

The anti-pollution committee of the Oneida Lake Association contacted me about the problem and met several times at my home to discuss the situation in 1961. We decided that, since the entire lake was affected, all four counties bordering it should be involved. I sent invitations to their chief political officers, and finally a meeting was held at my home in August. The outcome was a proposal to hire a resident engineer to advise people, communities, and businesses building new sewage facilities along the lake. The engineer's salary was to be paid equally by the state and the four counties involved: Onondaga, Oswego, Madison, and Oneida.

In time, the engineer was hired, and considerable progress in reducing the effluents of raw sewage has been made. The algae continues to be a problem, however, and experts have concluded that the entire water shed of the lake needs sewage treatment in the not-too-distant future.

The expertise I gained in these meetings was useful later, when, in 1965, I was asked to serve on the Onondaga Lake Scientific Council. This lake, bordering Syracuse, had at that time been severely polluted for many years. The main polluter was the Solvay Process Company, a division of the Allied Corporation, which had dumped tons of chemical wastes into Onondaga Lake. Raw sewage emptied into the lake from parts of Syracuse and from several small villages nearby. By 1965, political pressure for a cleanup was mounting, so, along with seventeen scientists of note from the area, I was asked to volunteer my services in this cause. In 1966, our council finalized its report, "An Environmental Assessment of Onondaga Lake and its Major Contributory Streams," and presented it to John Mulroy, the Onondaga County Executive who had convened the council. The report was good experience for all of us who served on the council; but, although several of our suggestions were acted upon, no thorough cleanup of the lake has yet taken place.

Over my years as health officer for the Town of Constantia, I was involved in many areas of progress in public health. To indicate the range of these, I shall quote a few excerpts from minutes of the board of health:

In 1936, "The quarantine of Scarlet Fever patients was reduced from 28 to 21 days."

In 1943, "Five dollars was authorized to be paid to Crawford Peck for burying a dead pig."

In June 1955, "Dr. Brown reported on the success of the Polio Immunization Clinic."

In October 1964, the question of a sewage disposal system came up for discussion. "It was concluded that the cost would be prohibitive for a small village the size of Cleveland."

In September 1965, "Dr. Brown stated he had received a supply of 160 doses of measles vaccine from the Federal Government and that he would conduct a clinic to dispense the prophylactic vaccine in the near future."

In December 1969, "Dr. Brown stated that the Kindergarten children in our area were the first group to receive the new vaccine to protect them against Rubella (3-day Measles)."

Not all my work as health officer consisted of committee work. I was often called out to provide medical services related to my public duties. Once such a call almost cost me my life, when I was asked to give a psychiatric evaluation of a local man named Dudley.

Dudley lived with his family on the lower road in the Village of Constantia. He was in his early forties and earned his livelihood as an itinerant carnival worker. In the winter, he fished through the ice on Oneida Lake to earn a few extra dollars.

One day in the mid-sixties, the school census officer, making her usual count of the upcoming children to be registered for kindergarten that year, was puzzled when she visited the Dudley home. The expected four-year-old was nowhere to be found, and she could discover no good reason for him to be missing. She reported the matter to the school authorities, who in turn notified the Bureau of Criminal Investigation through the Sheriff's Department of Oswego County.

The Bureau sent out an investigator, a Cleveland resident named Ben Butler, to look into the case. He extracted from Dudley the grisly admission that his four-year-old son had died and that Dudley had put his body in a potato sack, dug a hole near the house, and buried him. The remains were dug up, and Dudley was arrested and taken to the county jail for arraignment.

The judge then called me up and asked me to make a psychiatric evaluation of Dudley in my capacity as health officer of the Town of Constantia. He asked me to commit Dudley to Marcy State Hospital, a mental institution near Utica, for investigation of his mental state. I agreed, and about two hours later Dudley was brought to my office by two deputy officers. I examined him, talking with him for about twenty minutes. I determined that he was mentally unstable and needed care

149

and treatment. Therefore, I completed health officer papers committing Dudley to Marcy State Hospital for examination and testing over thirty days.

Dudley didn't stay for thirty days, however. On his twenty-ninth day there, some friends visited him and convinced the officer of the day at the hospital that one day less wouldn't make a difference. They had rented a car and would take him home, they said. The Sheriff's Office in Oswego was supposed to be notified when Dudley was released. Moreover, Dudley was supposed to have been returned to jail, after which the judge would determine his future in the light of the hospital findings on his mental condition. The doctor on duty didn't know these things or realize the seriousness of the case; he released Dudley into the custody of his friends.

The morning after Dudley was released from Marcy State Hospital, I got a call from his neighbors: Dudley had a shotgun and was on his way to Cleveland to "get" me for committing him to Marcy! I immediately called the sheriff's department, and they dispatched a number of state troopers to intercept Dudley. Luckily for me, they caught him on Route 49, near Bernhards Bay, only three miles from Cleveland! It was a close call.

As time went on, I found out just how close a call it really was. At his trial in Oswego, Dudley was convicted of unlawful burial. The cause of his son's death could not be determined, however, so no further charges were brought, and the judge sentenced him to banishment from New York State. The doctors at Marcy had determined that Dudley was not psychotic, but in my opinion he certainly had a psychopathic personality.

My encounter with Dudley was certainly the most dramatic episode in my duties as a health officer. I will never forget that telephone call, warning me that Dudley was coming for me with a shotgun!

In addition to my official paid duties, I continued to keep up affiliations with the wider medical world in a variety of ways. I remained a member of the American Academy of General

Practice (later the American Academy of Family Physicians) and its state and county branches. I also continued my membership in the Madison County Medical Society, serving as its president in 1954-1955, and later as chairman of its legislative, malpractice, and insurance committees. I continued to serve as an alternate delegate to the New York State Medical Society and later as the delegate of the Fifth District Branch of the M.S.S.N.Y., and as the Madison County Medical Society delegate to the four-county committee. Later I became chairman of that committee and, later still, a member of the planning board that, in the sixties, constructed the building housing the Central New York Academy of Medicine in New Hartford, New York, and became its president in 1971.

Except for one two-year period, I have served on the board of directors of the Syracuse Medical Alumni Association since 1970. In that capacity, I helped encourage the Clinical Preceptorship Program at the Syracuse Upstate Medical Center. This program was designed to give medical students first-hand exposure to an office practice in the field of their choice by sending them to spend a week or more observing and learning in the private offices of practicing doctors. These doctors would serve as preceptors, introducing students to the realities of private practice through exposure to actual patients.

Generally, students would be given this opportunity in their sophomore year, after having completed a course in physical diagnosis. I first took part in this program in 1971, when a student interested in general practice lived with our family for six weeks. For many years thereafter, I took a student or two every spring for a week or more. I greatly enjoyed this one-to-one approach to teaching office practice, and my patients seemed to enjoy it also. They would aid my visiting students all they could; not one ever failed to cooperate. I also admired my students' enthusiasm and aptitude. If the skills exhibited by these young people are indicative of the store of knowledge prevailing among their generation, I don't think our country has anything to worry about.

As a result of my participation in this program, I became an assistant professor in the Department of Family Practice at the Upstate Medical Center, and at my retirement I was named Emeritus Professor. During these years I also worked with the admissions committee, interviewing applicants to our medical school. Over the years, I gave up many Thursdays (my day off) to this interviewing process, presenting my observations and opinions to the admissions committee for their final decision.

Ever since my days as a medical intern at the St. Lawrence State Hospital, I have been interested in mental health. So when in 1967 I was asked by our town supervisor, Mrs. Grace Morse (Harold Morse's widow), whether I would like to join the newly created Board for the Oswego County Mental Health Center, I immediately said yes.

Before 1965, there were no mental health facilities in Oswego County. The County Health Association, under Bee's early leadership, was extremely active in pressing for mental health services, however, and after commissioning a study of the issue, the Board of Supervisors for Oswego County formally approved the formation of a Mental Health Board. A board of lay people was appointed, a director, Dr. J. Anthony Gillett, recruited, and in April 1965 the Oswego County Community Mental Health Clinic opened for business. To comply with mental health regulations a doctor of medicine was needed to serve on the board, and so I was asked to join it in early 1967.

The clinic prospered—so much so that it soon outgrew its living quarters. With the approval of the Board of Supervisors, the Mental Health Board set about the task of having a completely new center built in Oswego. Dr. Gillett was very active in this endeavor, soliciting grant money from the National Institute of Mental Health for the purpose, and by June 1973, the new center was treating patients.

Soon, however, Dr. Gillett was having difficulties with the center's staff, especially its president, J. B. Kelly, Jr. Mr. Kelly seemed to disagree with Dr. Gillett on almost every issue and soon convinced most of the members on the Mental Health Board that Dr. Gillett should be dismissed. My own feelings were that Mr. Kelly's dislike was personal and that Dr. Gillett would prove himself an effective director in time.

At that time, however, several inspections of our center by a team from the N.I.M.H. showed that criteria on our part were lacking, further undermining Dr. Gillett's prestige. Finally, in October 1973, a special meeting was held, and Dr. Gillett was asked to resign by December 31. I believe I was the lone dissenter on the board.

A new director, Murphy Berger, took over in April 1974. He had worked for several counties in southeastern New York State in the mental health field, and he seemed well-qualified. Before long, however, he, too, seemed to be having difficulties with the staff. Moreover, because he could not meet the regulatory criteria set up by N.I.M.H., its representatives threatened to withdraw funding. Soon the news media began printing all sorts of derogatory stories about the center. Things did not improve over the months that followed; the bitterness between the office management and the staff grew.

Through all these vicissitudes, however, the center continued to treat people in the area, and progress among its patients was steady. For me, the years I spent on the board turned out to be one of the great learning experiences of my life; it was stimulating to see that modern medicine could help not only the body but the mind.

Conflict among those running the center continued, however, and by early 1975 it was clear that Berger's hold on the situation was failing. In the light of this deterioration, the Board of Supervisors, after conferring with our board, finally fired him in the middle of May. At the end of June, I left the board with mixed feelings, having served out my tenure. I continued to watch developments with interest, though, and after a period of turmoil the center finally seemed to settle down. In June

1979, it was renamed the Alvin Krako Comprehensive Community Health Center, in honor of the chairman of the Oswego Board of Supervisors who spearheaded the restoration of the center to its rightful position in the community.

Of all the "medical" organizations I belonged to, the one I derived the most pleasure from was the American Medical Tennis Association. Tennis had always been my sport; in my teens I was fortunate enough to win some local tournaments, and on one occasion I, along with another youngster, represented New York State in a national tournament. I played for Syracuse University as its number-one team player during my college years and represented Syracuse in several intercollegiate events. Then for thirty years I had little time for the sport, playing only occasionally on vacations or my days off. When the A.M.T.A. was formed in 1967 to promote fitness among members of the medical community, it seemed a perfect opportunity to rejoin the sport on a regular basis; I became a charter member.

For many years thereafter, the association's annual Desert Classic tournament, held in Palm Springs, California, became the occasion for a yearly two-week vacation with Bee. In 1975, Terry became the administrator of the Maricopa County Hospital in Phoenix, Arizona, and Miner became the administrator of the Jewish Center for the Aged in St. Louis—very conveniently for us, their homes made nice stopping places en route to or from the Desert Classics! I also played less regularly at other A.M.T.A. events, winning several trophies over the years. Getting back into tennis gave me great satisfaction, but an even greater source of satisfaction was the camaraderie that developed among the association's members, a fellowship based on not one but two great loves, tennis and medicine.

Medical associations were not the only ones claiming my attention over these years, however. Bee and I both loved the area in which we lived, and we wanted to do our best to improve it. Therefore we both took a hand in many community affairs. We both served on local school boards, I on the board of the early Union School in Cleveland and Bee, later, on the board of the new Central Square centralized school system, a position she held for eleven years. I also served on the executive board of the local Boy Scout council, a position I still hold. The meetings are always stimulating; it is gratifying to see presidents of banks and industries, chairmen of large corporations, and other community leaders spending so much of their time, effort, and money to help the youth of the community. In 1978, I was greatly honored when the Hiawatha Council of Onondaga County gave me the Silver Beaver Award, the highest honor in scouting that a council can bestow on a volunteer. Finally, I helped Bee in her all-out effort to organize a local chapter of the American Field Service.

Bee, meanwhile, was at least as busy as I was. She became president of the Madison County Medical Auxiliary and its legislative committee chairman. She became the New York State Medical Auxiliary's Fifth District Councilor, and chairman of the New York State Fair Exposition, Public Relations, National Bulletin, and Rural Health Committees. As noted earlier, she became president of the Oswego County Health Association and was responsible for its reorganization, a feat which in turn helped lead to the formation of the Alvin Krako Comprehensive Community Mental Health Center and, later, to the formation of a nurses association and the Department of Health. She served on the state boards of the Tuberculosis, Respiratory Disease, and Heart Committees, and became a director of the Oswego County Cancer Society. She was also an active member of the Syracuse General Hospital Auxiliary and served as Matron of the Cleveland Chapter of the Order of the Eastern Star.

We also had commitments related to our religion. We were both active members of the Syracuse chapter of the American Jewish Committee and would drive to Syracuse often to attend meetings. We attended Friday night services at the Temple Society of Concord, and I served twice, in the 1950s and 1970s, on its board of trustees. Likewise, Bee became the Temple Sisterhood

HOUSE CALLS

President in 1964, and in 1978 she was elected the first female vice-president of the Temple Society of Concord. She also held memberships in the council of Jewish Women, Hadassah, and the Auxiliary to the Jewish Home of Central New York.

In the 1970s, I also became interested in the Syracuse chapter of the Anti-Defamation League of B'nai Brith, an organization formed to eradicate prejudice, bigotry, and discrimination against all citizens. This purpose stirred my emotions deeply, and I made many trips to Syracuse to hear the league's speakers and meet fellow members. In 1974, I was asked to become the chapter's chairman, a position I accepted as an honor. Soon after being elected, however, the league's professionally staffed upstate office was closed for financial reasons, leaving me with little to do. I did put together a workshop in 1978 on teaching the Holocaust in secondary schools, and I kept members informed about several cases involving possible anti-Semitism.

All these many and varied commitments kept Bee and me on the go constantly. At times it seemed we saw each other only in passing, especially when my practice was also busy and I had to spend nights out delivering babies or attending emergency cases. There were times when we both wondered if the tasks we had set ourselves were worth it.

In the early sixties, however, our community answered our doubts with a resounding "Yes!"

First, in 1962, Bee received a letter from Henry Keller, publisher of the *Post Standard* (Syracuse's morning paper), to say that she had been chosen as the newspaper's Woman of Achievement in Citizenship for that year. I had initiated the process by visiting Alice Keegan, the women's editor at the *Post Standard* to ask if Bee had a chance at the honor. Our neighbors on the North Shore were the people who ensured that she was chosen. They sent many letters to the paper, urging consideration of Bee and relating all the things she had done for the community.

Bee was thrilled at being chosen, crying with happiness at the news. Pictures and articles, radio interviews, and letters and phone calls of congratulations poured in, culminating in a luncheon in February 1963, at which all the twelve women of achievement had their accomplishments read out from the podium. It was a proud day for Bee and all her family.

On October 10, 1963, it was my turn to flush with pride and embarrassment. In celebration of my twenty-fifth year as a doctor on the North Shore, Cleveland decided to give me a party. My secretary, Edna Saunders, along with several other friends and neighbors, decided to accord me this honor, holding a community reception for me in the Cleveland elementary school.

I shall never forget that day. Articles about me appeared with my picture in several newspapers and in my college fraternity magazine. About five hundred well-wishers attended the reception, including many of the babies I had delivered, some in turn bringing their own babies. My first delivery in private practice, Mrs. Corsette, and her seven-month-old son, my first second-generation baby, were both there. Hoopey came from Mansville for the party, and Neal and Stephen made it home too. But perhaps the thing that touched me most deeply that day was the essay Miner had sent for the occasion.

WHAT IS A FAMILY DOCTOR?

He is the man who makes house calls day and night, in city or in country, rain or snow, to minister to the ills of dad, mother, grandfather, grandmother, sister, or baby brother. He is the man who comforts the anxious relatives when a dear one is seriously ill or is having an operation (which he himself may be doing). He is the man who brings joy and happiness to the home by delivering the new baby. He is the man who patiently talks over the problems of the teenage son or daughter. He tries to patch up mom and dad when divorce seems the only solution. He fixes Susie's broken arm, treats Johnny's pimples, brings dad through his coronary. Along with the minister or priest, he is the spiritual as well as the medical advisor for the whole family. It is his special knowledge of the spiritual, emotional, environmental, and physical characteristics of his patients which makes his services so vitally necessary in the field of medicine

HOUSE CALLS

today.

In short, he is a man dedicated to the art of healing and of serving mankind without regard for personal feelings or biases. Many times he has to sacrifice his own pleasures, desires, and wishes to leave his home and go to help a person in need at a moment's notice.

How do I know all this is true? My father is one. He has lived this sort of life for twenty-five years and, from his smile of satisfaction, has loved every moment of it. In fact, he thrives on being a "country doctor."

Many illustrative words of thanks can be expressed time and time again for these many years of community service. But I can only think of two—Dad, you've been a true Doctor and an inspiration not only to the community but also to me, my wife and brothers, and to everyone who has known you.

Sorry that we can't be with you for your twenty-fifth anniversary, but I'll guarantee that we'll be there for your fiftieth.

Eleven
Bee's Illness

In early 1966, Bee and I were making plans to visit Gerda, her husband Robert, and their family in Vienna and then go on for a tour of Israel. I purchased our plane tickets for the trip and made hotel reservations in London, where we were to spend two days before going to Vienna. Gerda made the remaining reservations for us.

In her letter to us dated March 6, Gerda wrote that after our stay in London, we would arrive in Vienna on April 10, then, after four days there, we would spend three days in Athens, then arrive in Tel Aviv on April 17. She told us that she had made all the reservations for an independent tour by private car, including a day in Jerusalem on April 25 for Independence Day. Then we should be ready to leave for our flight home on April 29.

But Bee had not been feeling well, complaining of easy fatigue, stomach distress, and chest pains. She was under considerable stress, so I assumed that the cause of these symptoms was her activities, and I thought that a holiday would be just the thing for her. To be sure, I had her examined and X-rayed by Drs. Irving Ershler and Theodore Perl, two very competent physicians in Syracuse, and also by Dr. Herbert Bauer, a gynecologist who had just taken over Dr. Monroe Rosenbloom's practice. They all came up with essentially normal findings; therefore, we were physically cleared to proceed on our trip. But Bee still complained of anterior chest pains and began to wonder out loud whether she was turning out to be a neurotic.

So Bee and I left Cleveland April 7 for our holiday. My nurse, Doris, drove us to the Syracuse Airport late in the morning, where we checked our baggage through to London. We were met at Kennedy Airport by Neal, his wife Carol, and their daughter Courtney. After about two hours waiting for our flight, we said our good-byes and were in the air on our way to London. There we toured the city visiting St. Paul's Cathedral, London Bridge, Trafalgar Square, and other tourist attractions. We did some shopping. We saw the play *Guys and Dolls* at the Savoy Theatre.

Soon we were on our way to Vienna, where we were met by Gerda and Robert at the new and modern Schweket Airport. They gave us their bedroom while they used the bedroom in their basement apartment. A party was held in our honor, and we met many interesting Viennese people, all of whom seemed to be economically well off, dressed very well, and enjoying their lives. Bee and I were able to shop by ourselves downtown, and I got along with the German-speaking people fairly well with my knowledge of Yiddish. When I told the taxi driver to take us to *Fir und fersich Hasenauerstrasse* I felt very accomplished. Gerda took us to some of the museums, we ate outdoors in the Stadtpark, enjoyed the opera, and Robert took us one evening to the famous *Drei Hussars* restaurant for dinner.

We did the usual sightseeing in Athens and spent three delightful days there. In Israel our personal guide drove us daily from our home base at the Sheraton Hotel in Tel Aviv to sites all through Israel. Except for two occasions—when we visited Haifa and flew to Eilat on the Red Sea—we were able to return each night to our hotel.

One of these tours was a day's trip to the Dead Sea. On the way we took a short rest at Beersheeba and then proceeded on past Sodum, where we viewed the large potash plants, and past the pillar of rock depicting Lot's wife, and the Massada. We stopped at a large bath house along the way where some of the people, including Gerda and Robert, rented swimming suits and floated in the saline water of the Dead Sea, the lowest point in the world. We finally stopped at Ein Gedi at the northern end of the Dead Sea, a watering place where we could rest, have some lunch, and relax. While we were sitting and having lunch, the guide asked if we would like to walk up to an Oasis, about ten minutes walking time. Not wanting to miss anything, we volunteered, and off we went. By this time it was extremely hot, and the walk didn't take ten minutes, it took about an hour. It was over sand and small hilly areas, and the Oasis turned out to be a small waterfall with a pond for bathing. When we returned to Ein Gedi to resume our return trip to Tel Aviv, Bee almost collapsed, and she had difficulty breathing for a few minutes. We all blamed this on the long walk and heat. We were each glad to get back to our hotel. By this time Bee had rested and was feeling all right.

The remaining days of our Israel holiday were uneventful, and our return flight was prolonged and extended over five hours, because all the Eastern coastal airports were fogged in, and our plane circled and circled before landing. We were both exhausted when we finally arrived home at 1 A.M. All this time Doris waited for us.

Soon we were back to our usual routines, but we were also making plans for Terry and Janis's wedding, which occurred on August 6 in Silver Spring, Maryland. It turned out to be a wonderful weekend and another holiday not only for us but also for the whole family. After their honeymoon, the Terry Browns took up residence in New York City not far from the Neal Browns.

Before this event Stephen graduated from high school with his class on a hot June day. So we were kept busy most of the fleeting days.

During the Labor Day weekend, the New York City Browns

spent their weekend with us, and it was a great feeling to have our whole family together. All we boys played golf together, we all went out in our boat, and they all enjoyed my outdoor cooking expertise.

A few days later, we packed up Stephen and drove him to Boston where he became enrolled in Grahm Junior College. Johnny Butler, Stephen's closest friend, came along with us since he was starting his second year there. Johnny was a great help and aided Steve with his orientation in no small way. After settling Steve in his living quarters and bidding our bittersweet farewells, we began our journey back to Cleveland. Bee and I were tired from the driving and unpacking, so we drove to Albany and took a room overnight at the Howard Johnson Motel. Up early the next morning and somewhat refreshed I drove us back to Cleveland and began treating patients in my office, delivering babies, and assisting at all kinds of surgery. However, Bee began to have symptoms of an upper respiratory infection that seemed to persist in spite of the usual medication prescribed for these illnesses. She saw Dr. Ershler again, and he reassured her once more that nothing serious could be found on examination. But she continued with her upper abdominal and chest pains.

Later in the month we decided to go to a convention of the American Academy of General Practice in Boston. It was to be held in early October and would give us an opportunity to visit Stephen. He got us reservations at the Commonwealth Motel, not far from Fenway Square, where he had his classes, and not far from the convention headquarters. I thought this would be a relaxing several days for Bee and would help her get over what we decided were allergic reactions. But it didn't turn out the way we had anticipated.

On the second day of the convention Bee felt worse, began to cough more, and was weak. She didn't feel up to attending any of the women's meetings but thought a walk out in the crisp, cool air would make her feel better. We began walking along Commonwealth Avenue and soon were passing by the reknowned Lahey Clinic. As an aside I said to Bee, "Maybe I ought to leave you here for a thorough work-up." Our lives would have changed if, indeed, I had gone through with this threat. But because Bee wasn't responding well, I decided to check out of the motel and get her home to Cleveland.

The following few weeks went along as usual except for her persistent hacking and coughing. One day she felt well, and the next day she didn't. However, she managed to attend her school board meeting and her monthly Sisterhood meeting. Although she had recently finished her tenure as its president, she still was taking an active part in it. As one of the fundraising projects in early November, the women of the Sisterhood were planning a fashion show, and the models were to be some of their own members. Bee was asked to be one. She was to model clothes for Flah and Company, a very high class fashionable women's shop in downtown Syracuse. On November 1, 1966, as we were having breakfast, she stated that she hadn't felt so well in a long time and that she was going to Flah's in Syracuse to try on clothes for the fashion show. I had to be at the Oneida City Hospital to assist Dr. William Hummer for surgery on one of my patients. She was going to drive in with her car, so we decided that she would have lunch in Syracuse after her fittings and that I would stop at one of the restaurants on my way home but probably would make it in time for office hours. She thought she would be home by three o'clock.

Bee drove into Syracuse and parked her car about one city block away from Flah's. As she started to walk toward the store, she began to feel uneasy and in about the middle of the block suddenly was seized with a burning, sharp pain across her anterior chest region, associated with some shortness of breath. Bee thought she was having a "coronary" but wanted, at least, to get to Flah's. So she leaned against a building for a few minutes, caught her breath, and continued on her way. She was able to enter the store, and she walked a short distance when the seizure returned, but more severely. She tried to grab a counter, but instead collapsed to the floor, unconscious.

The manager of the store, Gordon Grananstein, was notified, and he immediately called for an ambulance. By the time it arrived, Bee had begun to come around and mumbled, "Son, Upstate—Son, Upstate." Believing she had a son at Upstate, the ambulance crew took her to the Upstate University Hospital for treatment where Miner, an administrator assistant there, was informed of her admission.

It was about 11:30 A.M. by then, and I arrived home shortly afterward. Mr. Grananstein tried to contact me at Oneida and my office. I returned his telephone call immediately, and he told me that he thought Bee had lost her balance and hit her head on the floor and that he sent her to the hospital as a precaution. Then I called Miner, who was with his mother, and he told me that she was comfortable. I told him to contact Dr. Ershler and that I was leaving immediately for Syracuse. When Miner contacted Dr. Ershler, he at first wanted Bee transferred to the Community-General Hospital, across the city, where he was chief of staff. But, because I was on my way to Upstate, he decided to examine her there and then determine with me what procedures would be taken.

When I arrived at the Upstate Hospital, Bee was lying on a stretcher in a holding area of the Emergency Room. Dr. Ershler was there, and as I approached he said, "Marv, listen to her heart." For the first time I took out my stethoscope and carefully listened to the sounds of the heart lying in Bee's chest. And I turned away, scared. The second sound over the aortic area was barely audible, very weak, and the first sound was displaced by a murmer which radiated to her neck, and there also was a murmer over the apex of the heart which seemed to arise from the aortic area. These findings to me meant an advanced aortic stenosis, a severe narrowing of the outlet of the aortic valve. Dr. Ershler agreed and then told me that he had found the aortic murmer on several occasions, but thought that it was a congenital, functional abnormality that would cause no special difficulties. He agreed to have her worked up at Upstate, and so we waited until 8 P.M. for a bed to be opened up for Bee. By this time she was fairly comfortable, had drunk a large milkshake, was taking fluids, and had had a light supper.

After seeing her comfortable in bed for the evening, I left for home. Testing and thorough examinations were performed on Bee the following morning.

Driving home, I felt guilty and depressed about Bee's plight. Where had I gone wrong? Why didn't I, as a physician, examine and listen carefully to her heart before? But, after all, she had gone through four pregnancies and a miscarriage and had been examined by numerous competent physicians, and none had ever informed me that she had a heart murmur. Sure, Dr. Ershler knew she had an aortic murmur, but he presumed it was functional and would not give her any serious trouble and so did not, until now, inform me of this finding. He also informed me that he had been following many such murmers in some of his seventy- and eighty-year-old patients and that they functioned very well without signs of heart failure. Then what had happened so quickly to Bee's heart? Yes, she'd had scarlet fever in childhood, but if she had developed rheumatic heart disease as a complication, it surely would have been easily picked up long before now. All these questions and thoughts kept going through my mind, and produced a restless and somewhat sleepless night for me.

Early the following morning I checked with Miner at the hospital and found that Bee had had a fair night and was undergoing X-ray and blood examinations. After my afternoon office hours, I drove to the hospital and met with Dr. Ershler to go over Bee's charts, review the results of her tests, and determine what course of treatment would lie ahead. The important intensified fluoroscopic screen examination showed that there was heavy calcification in her aortic area. Dr. Ershler's opinion was that Bee should have an aortic valve replacement.

He told me what options we had, since there were only a handful of surgeons performing heart valve replacements in the United States at that time. He mentioned going to Houston, Texas; Rochester, Minnesota; Cleveland, Ohio; or Boston, Massachusetts. I had recently read an article on valve replacements written by Dr. Dwight E. Harken, of Boston, and also had heard him give a lecture on the same subject, during which he stated that, on March 10, 1960, he had been the first surgeon to design and implant into the human the caged-ball valve in the subcoronary position. From his lecture and also since he had the courage to perform such surgery for the first time, Dr. Harken inspired my confidence, so my opinion was to go to him. Dr. Ershler agreed, called Dr. Harken's office in Boston the next morning, and arranged for him to examine Bee on November 9, 1966.

Bee was discharged from Upstate and she rested at home, taking nitroglycerin at times to relieve her chest pain, for her appointment on the ninth. By this time our families, the boys, and Gerda were all being notified of recent developments. And I got my medical books out and studied up on aortic stenosis. Most of my information was obtained from Dr. Charles K. Friedberg's book *Diseases of the Heart*, published in 1949. Here are some of the important features of this unusual disease:

- Rheumatic calcific aortic stenosis is frequently associated with rheumatic disease of other valves; non-rheumatic form is much more apt to be an isolated valvular lesion. In advanced cases the valve cusps, ring, and commissures are entirely converted into a nodular stony mass, and an etiologic diagnosis may be difficult or impossible.
- The frequency of sudden death in calcific aortic stenosis has been repeatedly noted, and may occur with or without cardiac failure.
- The occurence of angina pectoris or *syncopal attacks* is unfavorable. *The occurence of death in aortic stenosis after an episode of snycope, or collapse, is on an average nine months later.*

With this information before us, there was no doubt in my mind what had to be done, and quickly. Before I took Bee home from the hospital we had a serious discussion about the outlook of her disease. It was rather difficult to break the news to her, but she took it well, and simply said, "Let's get on with it, and whatever happens, we've had such a good life together. It can't be taken away from us."

Back to Boston for our third time in two months we approached Dr. Harken's office with fear and trepidation. Would his opinion agree with ours? Well, we'll see.

It seemed strange to us that we had to reach the waiting room of his office by walking up a flight of about twelve stairs. Then, when we were seated, one of the patients there remarked, "You ought to see Dr. Harken's patients run up those stairs after receiving a heart valve replacement." And I thought, "In the future, will Bee be able to perform this feat?"

Finally Bee and I entered his private office. This tall, somewhat husky man in his middle fifties with thinning reddish hair and a kind, ruddy face, greeted us warmly, adjusted two chairs in front of his desk, seated Bee, and then sat down in his own chair to begin his history taking and examination. From the start he exuded confidence in both of us, and he literally held us in the palms of his hands. After he concluded his work he stated that Bee, without question, should have an aortic valve replacement.

He informed us that he was committed to be in South Vietnam for the State Department during December, but that Bee could enter the Mt. Auburn Hospital in Cambridge, Massachussetts on January 2, 1967, for further examinations with the prospect of surgery to follow. She was to go home, live an extremely quiet life, and take digitalis regularly and nitroglycerin when needed, so that, as Dr. Harken wrote in his letter to Dr. Ershler, "she can convert this rest period and inadvertent delay into strategic treatments to her advantage."

When we arrived home for the almost two-month waiting

period, word spread rapidly in the north shore and, it seemed, throughout the medical community, our religious community of Syracuse, and so many other places that have touched our lives. The telephone kept ringing, and the mail began to mount, all wishing Bee well and good luck. Open heart surgery was comparatively rare at this time, and replacing a diseased valve within the heart with a man-made one made one marvel at what surgeons could perform. More medical miracles were yet to be done, and they were on the horizon.

Bee was now fairly comfortable, but any undue exertion caused her to have chest discomfort and some shortness of breath. And I listened carefully to the sounds of her heart every day. Bee's sister, Jacqueline Kosoff, spent some time with us, doing the cooking and keeping Bee company until I was able to obtain people to help out. Bee lived in night clothes and bathrobe most of this time, but she got dressed frequently, which made her feel more human. She read and watched television. Some days friends would drop in for short visits, and they would always give what encouragements they could to lift up Bee's spirits. Bee slept with her head elevated on a special pillow, and often during the night when her breathing became quiet as a whisper, I would gently put my ear on her chest to be sure her heart was performing. The time went very slowly.

I recall one day during the first week in December when Bee had a very bad day and complained of more than the usual chest pain, increasing dyspnea, and cough. She was in considerable distress. Listening to her heart, the second sound over the aortic area was practically absent, and the murmur replacing the first sound came through weaker. I called Dr. Ershler's office but found that he was at a clinical meeting of the American Medical Association in Houston, Texas. I turned to Dr. Asher Black, who was practicing cardiology in Syracuse. He said he would see Bee immediately, so we drove to his office on West Onondaga Street where he carefully examined Bee and checked her with an electrocardiogram. After we discussed Bee's condition, he felt

BEE'S ILLNESS

that she was in extreme danger and that waiting another month might be catastrophic. He thought that her disease was progressing rapidly and said that he would contact Dr. Donald B. Effler, the cardiac surgeon at the Cleveland Clinic, for us, because Bee could arrive there by plane in a few hours. With his hand on the telephone, I had almost given him the go-ahead, when I said, "Let's see if we can get in touch with Irv in Houston before we proceed, to get his opinion." We put the call through, and we were lucky to soon have Dr. Ershler on the other end of the line. He hedged but suggested we wait another day or two before changing our plans. Bee was in agreement, stating she had met and had full confidence in Dr. Harken and was willing to take her chances. The next few days proved the decision a right one since Bee actually seemed to be stronger with less pain, dyspnea, and cough. Both Drs. Black and Ershler soon conferred again, and each kept in touch with me in Cleveland. It seemed that the inner strength of Bee persevered and seemed to save her for her date of January 2, 1967.

From this episode onward, Bee spent practically all her time resting in bed while all of us counted the days. The Christmas and New Year holidays were soon upon us. Stephen was home from school, and the other boys and their wives were constantly calling us. On Saturday, the last day of 1966, Jacqueline Kosoff and her husband Edward came to see the new year in with us. It was quite an evening for us all, and although Bee remained in bed upstairs, the rest of us saw 1967 come in while sitting in our family room. The next day we would be leaving for Boston.

The first day of 1967 was a typical wintry day. It was cold, the ground was covered by several inches of snow, and more snow was forecast. The day was spent watching football games and packing. Bee was comfortable but anxious to get on the road. We would be driving to Albany, where we would stay overnight, and then the next day would drive to Boston and finally Cambridge where Bee would enter Mt. Auburn Hospital and Jackie and I would register at the Treadway Inn on Harvard Square.

HOUSE CALLS

After bidding our good-byes, we loaded the car, and Bee, Jackie, Steve, and I were soon on the New York Thruway, leaving Cleveland about 7:30 P.M. When I had driven about sixty miles and was in the vicinity of Herkimer, we ran into a terrific snowstorm that made driving very hazardous. The storm kept up all the way to Albany, and, at times, I almost had to come to a complete stop on the highway, because the visibility was so obscured. However, we finally made it to the Howard Johnson Motel in Albany, where two rooms were waiting for us. Jackie insisted Steve room with her, saying, "Maybe your Dad and Mother would want to be alone by themselves. They probably have lots to say." It almost sounded like we could be spending our last night together.

Monday turned out to be fair and free of snow. After a leisurely breakfast, we started out for Boston. We arrived there about 12:30 P.M. and took Steve to his dormitory to unload his baggage; then we went to a small restaurant just off of Fenway Square to eat lunch. We got directions to Mt. Auburn Hospital, where Bee was to be admitted between 1:30 and 2:30 P.M. I helped her fill out the admitting forms, and then she was taken to her room. After checking with the nurses on her station and seeing Bee comfortable in bed, Jackie and I drove a short distance and checked in at the Treadway Inn.

After breakfast the next morning we went to the hospital. Bee was scheduled to start having a barrage of testing. She was examined by Dr. Harken and several cardiologists, had blood drawn, and had several EKG's and routine X-rays taken. That evening Dr. Ellis, the cardiologist whom Dr. Harken consulted with, came in and had a long, fatherly talk with Bee about what the operation hoped to correct, her life afterward, what she hoped to accomplish with her life, and that she would soon encounter the most serious event in her life.

More tests were done the next day. All this time Bee was fairly comfortable, but her symptoms continued, now being relieved with specific medication. On her third hospital day she was scheduled to have a coronary arteriogram. In those days no cines were being done at the Mt. Auburn Hospital. After the dye was injected intravenously, many 10 by 12 inch X-rays were taken at the rate of five a second. As a result, the number of films shown to me by Dr. Schatzky, the roentgenologist, seemed to be endless. He explained them all and took his time, which I appreciated. The end result was that Bee's coronary arteries showed no special disease, which was the last requirement for her surgery to be permitted. The next day, Friday, we learned that the surgery was scheduled for the following Wednesday, January 11. I decided to drive back to Cleveland on Saturday to attend to several important matters, then I would return to Cambridge on Tuesday, after picking up Miner at Utica where he was visiting his in-laws. By this time Neal and Terry were notified to be present for their mother's surgery. And in her hospital room, we met Stephen's future wife, Elaine Fischer, who visited Bee on several occasions. They, too, would be present at the time of the surgery.

After a short visit in my office on Monday I left about 4 P.M. for Cambridge by way of Utica. Miner and I had a nice drive contemplating what life would have for us, what chances Bee was taking, and—with Harriet's pregnancy—how our family was growing. We drove as far as Framingham and slept in the Framingham Inn. Then, arising early, we ate a light breakfast and arrived at Bee's bedside about eleven o'clock. Jackie was there and seemed glad to see us. Bee was across the hall getting a bath that involved finishing off with an antiseptic solution all over her body; this procedure was done daily for five days before her surgery.

While Bee was out of her room, Jackie told us that Bee had had a couple of bad days, marked by chest pain and weakness. By this time Bee was even unable to walk across the hall by herself. When she returned to her bed I took out my stethoscope and was scared at what I heard—the first aortic sound was replaced by a low pitched *sh* sound, and the second sound was absent.

HOUSE CALLS

Two interesting but bittersweet events had occurred while I was gone. First, on Sunday morning while making his rounds, Dr. Harken walked into Bee's room and found her crying. "What are you crying about, lovely lady?" he asked. Bee replied, "I don't know," but kept right on crying. Dr. Harken immediately summoned a nurse and had her bring in a glass filled with chopped ice. "I'll be back in five minutes," he said. On his return he held a bottle of wine in his hand, uncorked it, and filled the glass of chopped ice with the wine. "And," turning to the nurse, he continued, "I want her to have the same every four hours."

The next day, our granddaughter Betsy's second birthday, Bee had the nurse wheel her down the hall where she could use the telephone to wish Betsy happy birthday, and to hear her voice.

We were registered at the Treadway Inn again. When Neal and Terry arrived in the afternoon, they had to get rooms nearby. Eddie had already arrived, and he and Jackie were occupying the room next to mine. Miner roomed with me.

That evening we all went to dinner at a restaurant on Harvard Square. I recall it very well, because it was a bitter cold evening and I felt sorry for the girls there dressed in their short, but fashionable for the time, dresses. I tried to eat but ate very little; I was thinking of Bee and what she had to go through the next day. Soon afterward I was back at the hospital. The surgery was scheduled for 7:30 A.M. the next day. Dr. Harken told me to have the family wait at approximately 2:30 P.M. in the hospital annex where he would explain to us the results of the surgery. Then I was alone with Bee for a few minutes. She said she was not afraid, that she had full confidence in her doctors, and that with her faith in God she would be all right. I kissed her goodnight and went back to the motel.

Miner and I had a rather sleepless night, but we managed to get some rest. Our group met in the lobby of the motel for breakfast about 9 A.M. the following morning. After breakfast the boys went for a walk and did some shopping. We agreed

BEE'S ILLNESS

to meet again in the same place at 2 P.M. I remained at the motel and tried to keep busy by reading. Soon after I'd had a light lunch, everyone met again, and we drove to the hospital annex to meet with Dr. Harken. We all were surprised to find Joan Wilson, Terry's high school girl friend, waiting for us. She had managed to get some time off from her job as a Pan Am stewardess and get a flight out of San Francisco to Boston, and here she was. She was a delight to our eyes, and, later on through our vigil, her spirit and laughter helped all of us get through those trying hours. We all shall never forget her encouragements and her "you can do it" attitude.

Well, 2:30 came and went, then 3 P.M., and then 4 P.M. We were all getting restless. I found out from one of the nurses, who went into the surgical suite for me, the reason for the delay.

There had been a devastating fire in a Naval base not far from Boston the night before, and there had been many burn casualties. The twenty units of blood that were ready for Bee's surgery were sent there to help in the treatment of the victims. Instead of getting Bee to surgery at 7:30 A.M., the laboratory was busy matching and cross-matching twenty fresh units of blood. This procedure took several hours, and the operation could not proceed without the blood which was needed to prime the heart-lung machine and to maintain the infusion throughout the surgery.

Therefore, instead of getting Bee to the operating room at 7:30 A.M., she was wheeled in and placed on the operating table at 12:30 P.M. I felt disturbed that we were not made aware of this change in plans, as I could have spent these hours with Bee. I was told later there was an administrative error in communication. Since the room we were in was comfortable, and the temperature outside was in the freezing zone, we decided to wait until the surgery would be completed.

The few hours remaining seemed like an eternity. I had Neal telephone Cleveland to inform Doris of the reason for the delay. Cleveland and the North Shore area of Oneida Lake were mobilized to spread word of Bee's surgery. I would call Doris, and she would call five other volunteers, who in turn would call five others until the community would be covered. Thus the immediate results of the surgery and progress of Bee's condition would be known almost up to the minute by the residents of the north shore communities. Also, phone calls were going on to my family and close friends at all times.

We estimated that Bee's surgery would be completed about 7:30 P.M., so we all became disturbed when 8:00 rolled around. Neal came to me with a worried look on his face and asked me the reason for the delay. I said that I didn't know. He left us and came back in a few minutes, looking scared and anxious. He had gone to the surgical suite, stopped a nurse there who had just walked out, and questioned her about the operation going on inside. She told him that they were having trouble and complications with the patient who had just had a valve replaced such that the bleeding from her heart could not be controlled.

With this information passed around we all sat in a subdued eerie silence, not knowing what to say, but I'm sure each one of us was praying for Bee in his or her own way. The silence was broken by Joanie's voice. "If anyone can do it, Bee can."

At about 8:45 P.M., Dr. Harken arrived, still in his bloodied operating gown, and with a worried look he told us of the operation—that Bee had survived the eight and a half hours on the table, that he watched over an hour for the bleeding from her heart muscles to subside, that he finally had packed the areas about the heart with oxy-cel and sent her upstairs to the intensive care unit, and that he hoped that she would be all right. He turned to me and said, "Marvin, you can come up and see Bee for a few minutes." On our way upstairs he went on, "I know you have seen many post-operative cases, but don't get alarmed when you see your wife and the many tubes and lines attached to her as well as a portable pulmonary machine. You see, when we took her off the heart-lung machine, her left lung failed to ventilate, and we had to intubate it with oxygen under positive pressure." I was prepared well because Bee was in bed, propped up, with tubes going all different ways and a bulky type of a lung respirator in place around her chest. After a few minutes there, Dr. Aloysius Chen, one of Dr. Harken's associates, told me he would remain at Bee's bedside through the night and would inform me of any undue changes.

I soon returned to the waiting family including our boys, Jackie, Eddie, and Joanie, and then we started to disperse to our motels. Bee's progress would be passed on to them immediately. Neal called Cleveland, relatives, and close friends with the information that the operation was over and that Bee's condition remained critical.

I stepped outside into the cold, fresh air, and I suddenly broke down, began to cry, wretched, and vomited. Everyone tried to console me, and when I settled down Miner and I went to our room at the motel. Soon Eddie brought in some sandwiches and soft drinks, which we ate rapidly, being the first food we'd had since noon. I went to bed with the telephone near my head, not knowing whether I would fall asleep before the phone rang or vice-versa.

Sleep won out, but at 7 A.M. I was awakened by the ringing of the telephone. It was Dr. Harken who told me that "Beatrice is responding satisfactorily" and that he had just finished performing an emergency tracheostomy that he hoped would allow her to get the needed air exchange into her lungs. I hurriedly dressed, went downstairs for doughnuts and coffee, and was soon at Bee's bedside. Miner remained at the motel. So, now, in addition to all the other tubes attached to Bee's body, another one was attached to the hole in her neck providing the needed oxygen to her lungs. However, her heart was stable, the bleeding was under control, and I now listened to her heart sounds for the first time with the new Harken modification Star-Edwards valve in place. It was noisy and clicking, but to me sounded like the most beautiful music in the world.

Bee was still in critical condition, but with good care and continuous monitoring, I could see more than a ray of hope for her recovery. From the hospital I went to the Western Union office and sent a cablegram to Gerda and Robert which stated, "Operation over. Mother critical. Will keep you further informed."

I hovered near the intensive care unit for the rest of the operative day. No other members of the family were allowed in to see Bee. She was heavily medicated, but every time I entered the unit she sensed my presence and by eye signs would recognize me. The family all went out to dinner again that evening, feeling somewhat relieved that the main procedure was over and looking forward with hope to Bee's total recovery. When I stopped back at the motel, there were several messages for me and several calls to make, all concerning Bee.

After my calls were completed, I went back to the hospital to see Bee again. It was now about 8:30 P.M. As I entered the intensive care unit and approached Bee's bed, I looked at the monitor recording Bee's heart beats, and I didn't like what I saw. Her heart was beating in a flutter-fibrillation rhythm, and she seemed to be in moderate respiratory distress. Dr. Chen was in attendance and gently pushed me away, stating that Dr. Harken would be in shortly and that they hoped normal rhythm would soon be reestablished. He suggested that I go back to the motel and told me he would call me with a progress report as soon as possible. I kept this to myself so as not to alarm anyone else. Miner urged me to undress and get into bed, but I just sat in the room, trying to watch television. At about midnight, Dr. Chen called and said that Bee was resting comfortably and that the heart was now in normal rhythm. I then confided to Miner what had transpired, and soon we were both in bed trying to get some sleep.

The next day Bee's condition was stable, and the doctors in attendance began to show some confidence in her recovery. Still the boys remained in Cambridge and gave me added support.

BEE'S ILLNESS

I visited Bee several times, and in addition to her eye signs I could now see the sides of her mouth curled upward in a Mona Lisa smile. Somehow Neal got in to see his mother in the afternoon. From his expression I could sense a worry and wonderment about the whole procedure that he was following and observing for the first time.

The boys began to leave on the third post-operative day. Eddie drove Miner back to Syracuse, and Neal and Terry returned to their homes in New York. Joanie had left the day before. Of course Stephen was nearby, and Jackie remained to keep me company. By this time the portable respirator was removed, and Jackie was now allowed to visit her sister.

During the next two days Bee showed satisfactory progress and was getting stronger. My calls to Cleveland, Syracuse, Utica and other communities were now easier for me to make. On the fifth post-operative day, Monday, I walked into the intensive care unit, and the charge nurse exclaimed to me, "Your wife is sitting up, and we are feeding her for the first time." And this is what I observed: The tube from the oxygen tank that had been attached to her tracheostomy was temporarily disconnected, and Bee was sitting in a chair next to her bed with the rest of the connections to her body dangling, but in place. She looked at me and gave me a smile and then reacted to commands given to her by the nurse. "Open your mouth, Mrs. Brown," and she would open her mouth as a spoonful of food was placed into it. "Now chew the food," and she would chew the food. "Now swallow," and she would swallow. Well, I was so proud of my wife, the zombie, as I observed her putting away a good-sized breakfast, that I knew she was going to make it. My feeling was also confirmed by Dr. Harken later in the day. After this visit to the hospital I returned to the Western Union office and cabled to Vienna the news, "Mother out of danger, progressing satisfactorily." At the same time I received a cablegram from Gerda and Robert addressed to Bee stating, "Wishing you a fast and complete recovery. Our thoughts are with you," And now cards and letters were arriving at the hospital, wishing Bee to get on the road to recovery. By the first week's end several hundred were being retained for her as they couldn't be brought into the intensive-care unit.

On my daily call to my family in Syracuse, my brother Maurice informed me that Rabbi Levy gave a beautiful prayer for Bee's recovery at the previous Friday night services. Also, Doris informed me that all the churches in the area had offered up prayers for Bee. These messages were very comforting and made me realize how wonderful real friends can be.

Jackie and I then started our routine. We generally rose, dressed, and were downstairs for our usual breakfast. I would often eat a large orange in my room before leaving. Then we would visit Bee at the hospital until lunch time. Back to the motel for messages and mail. Then back to the hospital until evening, when we would go out for dinner. We tried a different restaurant each night, but after several days we drifted back to the one or two that seemed to offer us the best meals.

On the sixth post-operative day, Dr. Harken suggested that I make rounds with him, stating that I'd been exposed to considerable stress, and since Bee was out of danger I could leave her in the mornings to spend some time with him visiting other patients. So he picked me up at 8:30 A.M. the next day, and away we went. He drove at a fast pace, and soon we were in the Peter Bent Brigham Hospital. I followed, or rather ran, after him as he seemed to fly through the halls, running up and down the stairways, going in and out of patients' rooms, giving his orders to the residents, keeping up a constant chatter to me and a Japanese surgeon who was visiting Boston. On one of these rounds we followed him as he had to make an emergency visit to the intensive care unit; when we arrived there I could see why Dr. Harken suggested Bee's surgery be done at the Mt. Auburn Hospital and not at the Brigham, because at the Brigham the I.C. unit was housed in a large basement room that seemed cold and non-professional, almost dungeon-like.

BEE'S ILLNESS

The next morning, Dr. Harken again picked me up, and we hurried to the Brigham again where Dr. Juro Wada was waiting. I found out that he came from Sapporo City and was the Professor of Surgery at the Sapporo Medical College and Hospital. He was a treat to be with, I enjoyed his company immensely, and he invited me to visit him for the upcoming Winter Olympic Games as his guest. That day, the American College of Cardiology was meeting in Boston, and Dr. Harken was operating in the surgical amphitheatre before a group of physicians. Before he entered the surgical floor he saw to it that Dr. Wada and I were allowed to enter the amphitheatre and be seated. The surgery being performed before us was an aortic valve replacement, and the operation had already been advanced by Dr. Harken's assistants to the stage where the man-made valve was to be seated and sewn into place. Being not only a great cardio-vascular surgeon but also a great showman, Dr. Harken began speaking into the microphone about what had transpired up to this point, and then he pointed upward to where I was seated and said, "Up there is Dr. Brown whose wife I operated on for a similar replacement only last week." I was embarrassed but happy to be in the temporary limelight because of Bee's surgery.

I made several more hospital rounds with Dr. Harken and during our visits learned to admire and respect him more and more. During these escapades Jackie was able to spend some time with her daughter, Susan, who was teaching elementary school on Cape Cod.

During one of our last hospital rounds I asked Dr. Harken if the pathology on the diseased aortic valve removed from Bee's heart had shown any definitive etiology. He told me that it was a solid mass of calcium with an orifice opening of 3 mm., or the size of a tip of a matchstick, and that whether it was due to rheumatic fever could not be determined. I then began to wonder about the beautiful workings of the human body and thought how Bee's vital organs could be maintained by a blood flow through such a tiny opening from her heart. Her surgery had been performed in the nick of time. And then I began to wonder again whether she would have been operated on sooner if I had been told of her aortic murmur by her physicians and could have been monitoring her for perhaps months or years before. This we shall never know, but at least Bee was now convalescing well and, barring any undue complication, could be home in Cleveland before long.

Bee was transferred to a private room on her eighth post-operative day. By this time all her tube connections except the drainage tube in her left chest region were removed, and before she left the I.C. unit the tracheostomy connection was also removed. She was eating well and beginning to get color back in her cheeks. She hated to leave the unit since she had become so dependent on the nurses there, all of whom were so dedicated and gave such wonderful care. However, the private nurses I was able to obtain for Bee were of the same calibre, and in her private room they equaled and continued the good nursing care.

On her ninth post-operative day Bee was allowed to walk down the hospital corridor. She grasped my arm and with my help shuffled along. We went about ten or fifteen feet when she looked up at me and said, "Marv, I'll never make it. Look at me, it's so long after my operation. I look so awful, and I'll never be any good." This took me by surprise, since it was one of the rare times I had ever heard Bee speaking in such a depressing manner. I tried to console her by saying, "Bee, this is only nine days after your surgery, and your progress has been so wonderful. You keep it up, and we'll still have many great years together ahead of us." This seemed to settle her down, and she grasped my arm tighter as we continued on.

The same day, Neal, Miner, and Terry returned with their wives to visit Bee, and they all seemed pleased. Neal also brought along my sister, Dorothy, who remained several days. Besides visiting together, they walked around Harvard Square, drove around Boston, and did more shopping. They remained two more days, and feeling their mother and mother-in-law would come along all right left for their homes in high spirits. Then Eddie returned to keep Jackie company, and on Sunday, January 22, I drove home to Cleveland. For the next three days I saw patients in my office, took care of my correspondence, and answered many, many telephone calls. During this time Jackie and Eddie kept Bee company and also kept me informed of Bee's daily progress. While at home I called Gerda and Robert to inform them of Bee's convalescence and then wrote them a letter detailing the operation.

On the 26th of January, I flew to Boston, rented a car, and remained until the 29th because I wanted to be back for a Red Cross Bloodmobile for Bee that was scheduled to be held at the Community Church in Bernhards Bay on January 30. That it was successful can be judged by two of the several notices placed in local newspapers:

MRS. BROWN HAS HEART SURGERY

Community Leader's Friends Join to Give Gift of Blood

The people living along the north shore of Oneida Lake and friends from outlying communities are going all out to give blood for one of the area's most active citizens when the Red Cross Bloodmobile visits the Community Methodist Church at Bernhard's Bay on Monday, January 30 from 3 to 6 P.M.

Mrs. Beatrice Brown, wife of Dr. Marvin Brown, Cleveland, is now recovering from open-heart surgery in a Cambridge, Massachusetts, hospital. Mrs. Brown, an ardent community worker, is described by those who know her best as "more than just a public-spirited citizen. She gave her heart and soul to the community—even to the point of endangering her own health." They ask one another, "What greater gift can one give than to lay down one's life in the lap of the community?"

Now the members of the communities strung along the northern shore of the lake are rallying around Beatrice Brown to show her that her work has not been in vain. They are giving the gift money cannot buy—a pint of blood. They have adopted the slogan, "Give

HOUSE CALLS

your pint of blood and bring a friend to give another." (Oswego Paper, 1/29/67)

NORTHSHORE BLOOD PROGRAM SUCCESS

We would like to extend a very grateful "thank you" to everyone who participated in any way during the Red Cross Bloodmobile visit to the North Shore on January 30th.

So many volunteers were involved it would be impossible to list each one individually. We would first like to thank the many donors. It was through your efforts that our first Bloodmobile was successful. There were 92 donors, 45 of whom were first time donors. The Red Cross was pleased to receive 83 pints of blood.

We would also like to thank the 10 local nurses who gave freely of their time after working at their regular jobs all day. Also the men of the community who helped to unload and reload the equipment and made themselves available to those who needed transportation. Thanks to the Cleveland Library Club for donating all the sandwiches for the canteen, also to the members of Cleveland Chapter #269 Order of Eastern Stars for donating all the cookies. The ladies of the community donated a delicious hot supper for the workers. Our thanks to the Town of Constantia Highway Department for plowing the church yard for parking, the many ladies of the community who worked at various jobs during the bloodmobile visit, especially those who worked in the canteen. They arrived at the church at 9 A.M. and cleaned the room and then worked in the canteen from 2:30 until all was back in order at 8:30. Last but not least to the two teenagers who were sitters. Each one did a wonderful job.

The Red Cross, Mrs. Marvin "Bee" Brown, and the committee who arranged the bloodmobile visit thank you all very much for your unselfish efforts. We should all be proud to be a part of such a wonderful community as the North Shore. Again, Thank You each and everyone. (Rome Daily Sentinel, 2/3/67)

I worked in my office the morning and early afternoon of January 30 then drove to Bernhards Bay to aid and observe the Red Cross Bloodmobile. It was a thrilling moment for me when I saw in large letters and emphasized by a large red heart the sign indicating the entrance to the basement of the community church where there were all kinds of activities going on. The sign read "BEE BROWN BLOODMOBILE DAY, Monday January 30th —3 P.M. to 6 P.M.—Bernhards Bay Church—Transportation and Nursery Care Provided." The Red Cross nurses were drawing blood from the accepted donors placed in the room on the many cots, other donors were being checked by volunteer local nurses; many volunteer women from local organizations were busy providing coffee, cookies, and other foods; baby sitters were doing their job; and Dr. Kent Jarvis came from Oswego to be the attending physician. A supper was prepared for all the volunteers and Red Cross personnel. I recall that a crew of Niagara Mohawk linesmen were working not far from the church, and one of them, a local husky Constantian, came in to donate his blood. After he finished his coffee, he soon returned with four others of his crew, all of whom also donated their blood.

About a week later the committee, led by Ned Jeffrey of Cleveland, received a letter from the Red Cross thanking the north shore committee for contributing 83 pints of blood. This contribution for a citizen of a small village shows what real Americanna can do when a crisis occurs or when a threat to existence might occur. Everyone seemed to pull together, and it gave me strength to see such a great display of the feelings that my people had in their hearts for my wife.

I returned to Boston three days later and went to the hospital to visit Bee. She was progressing satisfactorily, her sutures were all removed, and she was up and walking around, but at this time she showed two apparent complications. First, her vision on looking to the right was gone, and it was concluded that an embolus had occurred in her brain back of the optic chiasm during the coronary artery artiography. This right homonomous hemianopsia would be permanent, but she could live with it and would accommodate to it as time went on. Second, her right hand was weak, somewhat spastic, and partially numb. This was caused when the metal spreader placed in her open chest during the surgery produced undue pressure on the nerves going to her right hand. However, she was exercising the right hand which already was showing improvement.

Late that afternoon Dr. Harken came in the room with the good news that Bee would be discharged in two days. He carried with him a bottle of small orange-red pills. He told us there were a thousand pills in the bottle and to handle them like gold. The pills, he said, may or may not be Persantine tablets, which were under a controlled study by a Tufts research team trying to determine whether a side property of them would prevent platelet aggregation about the valve and whether they could be prescribed as an anticoagulant medication. Bee's bottle had the number 17 on it. Since each pill weighed 25 mg., the dose prescribed for her was four pills four times a day, or a total of 400 mg. a day. We found out later that she, indeed, was taking Persantine.

So on Saturday morning, February 4, Bee was taken to the hospital exit by wheelchair and, with help, got into Eddie's car. Soon, with Jackie in the front seat and Eddie driving, Bee and I were together again in the back seat, on the highway going west to Cleveland.

Bee's first remarks were thanks for all concerned, thanks for us, and thanks for her belief in God. While driving along she told us that Stephen had brought Elaine Fischer, a girl from Rochester who was a classmate of his, up to visit her on several occasions and that she probably would be our fourth daughter-in-law. She remarked how Elaine and her twin sister met Stephen, and that Stephen at first dated Gail, but then shifted his attention to Elaine, and that things were beginning to become serious.

I brought out the last letter I had received from Gerda dated January 20, 1967, in which she wrote that "life seems brighter ever since your call, and the letter, thanks for all the detail of the operation." She goes on to inform us that the telephone rang constantly, that they all prayed for Bee's recovery, and that "the second cable was one of the most beautiful and relaxing moments of my life." Also she wrote that she had taken sick

BEE'S ILLNESS

on the 11th, otherwise she "would be at our sides." We found out later that Gerda had had a miscarriage and was hospitalized herself at the time. The letter was signed "Many many kisses and our love to a new mother."

After riding for about three hours we arrived at the Howard Johnson Motel in Albany. Eddie had an interest in the motel, so he had a room ready for us where Bee could lie down for a couple of hours while we had lunch, and we would bring in some food for Bee. We appreciated being free guests for the time we spent there, courtesy of Eddie. Before long, Bee was back in Cleveland, and after I carried her upstairs and placed her in her own bed she almost broke down with happiness saying, "Oh, how good it is to be back in my own bed."

Jackie and Eddie remained for a few days. Jackie did the cooking and helped with the care of Bee. Eddie also kept Bee company while I resumed my practice. Janis was able to get away for two weeks, came up from New York, and took over the nursing duties. Friends and neighbors brought in all kinds of food, and we didn't lack for anything. Mary Lockerby kept up the housework and had our home and my office in spic-span condition. The following week I was able to obtain the services of Mrs. Herman from Bernhards Bay to take over the cooking duties, and, in her absence, Jennie Kessler, a neighbor, filled in for her. During Bee's first week at home Dr. Ershler came from Syracuse, both as a friend and as Bee's physician. He was happy to see Bee and after examining her gave all of us a good prognosis for her complete recovery. He also gave her an intramuscular injection of a large dose of gamma globulin as a precautionary measure, used at that time because of the large amounts of blood taken from many donors used in Bee's surgery.

Our household soon became almost normal again. Bee was ambulating well and by the time Janis left was getting dressed and walking fairly well up and down the long upstairs hallway. Between patients' visits in the office I would run upstairs to check on things, and Doris would make Bee comfortable before

HOUSE CALLS

she left for the day.

Dr. Harken requested Bee to send him a report of her progress after two weeks, and this is what she told him:

> I find each day I increase in strength and am more aware of the world around me than when I left Boston. I am taking the prescribed medications faithfully, and continue to do the breathing exercises. I am still unable to write because of the numbness in the two fingers in my right hand. Since the one radical change in my sight the few days before I left the hospital, my eyes remain the same. I am partially dressed, and go up and down the stairs once or twice a day.

Gerda wrote in her letter to us dated February 20, 1967, "Glad to receive Janis's letter and to hear all the good news. With a good nurse, how well the progress goes."

With Bee in the limelight our family almost neglected to follow the pregnancy of Harriet who by now was going into her sixth month. Bee was so happy about the oncoming birth remarking, "And look what I almost would have missed."

Bee was now getting stronger by the day. Her right hand was improving with exercise, and she gradually began to do more and more. However, she acted confused at times, and on one occasion when she got up to go the bathroom during the night she headed for the window instead of the bathroom. I got alarmed but then knew for sure that she was taking Persantine and not sugar pills. Since her first postoperative check-up with Dr. Harken was only a month away, I decided to watch her carefully until then and to continue with the experimental pills until we received an opinion from him.

I got a reservation at the Fenway Motor Hotel on Boylston Street in Boston for the night of March 16, 1967. A few days before we left for Bee's appointment I took her out for a drive. It was a cold wintry day; she dressed warmly, and she became so happy and exhilarated by the experience, since it was the first time in several months that we were out alone.

And so we arrived at our motel late in the afternoon, rested, and then had dinner in a nearby restaurant. During the night it began to snow, and it continued throughout the next day. After breakfast at the motel we took it easy until check-out time at 1 P.M., when we left for Dr. Harken's office for Bee's appointment.

There were several patients sitting in the waiting room, but before Bee got there I found out why the stairs were there. Like the Masters two-step test, Dr. Harken used a twelve-stair test. He watched Bee ascend them and in his report stated, "Mrs. Brown takes the flight of stairs in the office slowly but without distress." While waiting to be examined by Dr. Harken she had a conversation with one of the patients and told him that she wanted at least ten more years and hoped the valve would last that long. Dr. Harken was delighted with the continued progress Bee was making. He had her continue with the medication, but cut down the Persantine dosage to two pills four times a day. And he wanted to recheck her in about six months.

Being in Boston on March 17th, we found the business places quiet, as was the traffic on the streets. We could sense a holiday atmosphere. And when I learned that the small restaurant where we had lunch was featuring green beer, it finally came to me that this was St. Patrick's Day—a lucky one for us, as Bee's check-up with Dr. Harken turned out so well.

We left Dr. Harken's office about three o'clock and headed home, stopping several times to rest and relieve ourselves, eating supper in Albany, filling up with gas, and arriving home in Cleveland about 10 P.M. It was a tiring day for Bee, but she took it well, felt happy about it, and soon was in bed fast asleep.

Mrs. Hermann came the next morning but was only able to finish out the week. I was making plans to take Bee to Florida for ten days later in the month, but we still needed someone to take over the cooking and household tasks. Therefore, Bee contacted Leah Fuller, our old and dear friend who at that time was the housemother for the KKG sorority at Syracuse University, for help. It was a mid-semester break, so she came and spent it with us, cooking, shopping, and answering the telephone in the house when the office was not covered. She was seventy-one years old, but looked, moved, and seemed like a woman ten to fifteen years younger. Since the death of her husband, Ray, almost four years earlier, she had been living alone in a small house on Bridge Street in the village, and before her present position I was responsible for her being the housemother at my college fraternity.

Leah remained with us until Bee and I left for Florida, when she returned to her position at the sorority house. We had reservations at the Hollywood Beach Hotel in Hollywood, Florida, where we rested for ten days. Bee was taken about in wheelchairs at the airports, and also at the hotel for the first few days. The cooperation we received at all times was excellent. The weather in Florida was mild and warm, the sun was out most of the time, and Bee profited by it and gained considerable strength. We had breakfast in our room, lunches were served around the pool, and dinners were had in the main dining room. The vacation was good for me, too, and I was able to play tennis regularly, although my game was somewhat rusty.

While in Florida, Bee and I decided to offer Leah a proposition to come live with us, cook for us, shop for us, and literally to become a member of our family in return for a room and bedroom of her own. We wouldn't charge her anything and she wouldn't charge us anything. She would get free room and board in return for her services. This seemed like a reasonable and sound answer to both our problems: We needed help, and Leah was ready to give up her sorority job. She was very serious and responsible, but the girls there would pay no attention to curfew hours, and disciplining them meant little.

Jackie and Eddie returned to Cleveland to help out again when we returned from our vacation. Bee asked Leah to visit us in order to discuss our deal, which she did several days later. By this time Bee was getting dressed every day, coming downstairs, and beginning light work in the kitchen. Bee and Leah, who

BEE'S ILLNESS

were the best of friends, had a nice discussion, and the conclusions were satisfactory to all of us. Leah would come with us at the end of the college year, sometime in June. She would have the room off the kitchen for a sitting room, with her own couch, desk, television, and knicknacks, and a bedroom and bath upstairs. She would be free to come and go once Bee began to take over, but she would continue to cook, help with shopping, and, since she had her own car, would take Bee places until she might be able to drive herself.

On my first day off from practice I visited Wilson's Jewelry Store in Syracuse, and after consultation with Jerome Wilson decided to obtain gold cuff links with a diamond set in each. These would be gifts for Dr. Harken and his staff. Of course the pair of cuff links that I decided would go to Dr. Harken contained the largest of the diamonds. The other members of the operating team and the anesthesiologist all received similar cuff links with smaller diamonds. These cuff links were in lieu of a bill for services rendered, because Dr. Harken, speaking for himself and his associates, told me that he never sends a bill to physicians or physicians's family members whom he treats or operates on. However, even if a bill had been presented to me, I'm sure that gifts would have been rendered to Dr. Harken and his wonderful staff by Bee and me. But I must confess that then our gifts would not have been so lavish. When I received all the cuff links I indicated to whom each pair should be given. Bee enclosed a personal note with each pair, and I sent them along to Dr. Harken, together with a letter of thanks asking him to accept his and distribute the others. The following letter tells its own story.

May 3, 1967

Dear Bea and Marvin:

What elegant cuff links! What a delightful, touching, inspiring, sensitive letter you have written, Marvin.

189

HOUSE CALLS

All of us appreciate your generosity, thoughtfulness, and inspiring words more than you can know. I am sure I speak for the whole group when I say that we will think of you and lovely Bea whenever we wear these elegant cuff links.

Thank you for letting us come into your lives and be inspired by this participation.

Sincerely,
Dwight E. Harken, M.D.

On our March visit to Boston, since I had not received a bill from the hospital yet, I went up to the business office of the hospital and received the bill for Bee's hospital residence. This included thirty-two days, of which eight were spent in the intensive care unit, all her tests, X-rays, and examinations, all her medications, and general nursing care. The grand total was a little over $5,200, and most of this was covered by my sick and accident policy which I carried with my Four County Medical Group. Compared to today's prices we got a bargain, especially with Bee's continuing progressive convalescence.

Bee gradually improved in strength and vitality. By the time Leah moved into our home she was already assuming her kitchen duties and performing some household tasks. Leah and Bee organized their work schedules, and for the following nine years they seemed to be in harmony. Leah became a member of our family.

We kept returning to Boston for follow-up check-ups with Dr. Harken. He became very fond of Bee, and his remarks in his consultant letters often praised her for her physical attributes as well as her medical improvements. In his letter of February 8, 1968, he starts off with, "Our beautiful Beatrice Brown is here with her husband Marvin. . . physical examination reveals Beatrice to be looking extraordinarily healthy and glamorous." And in his discharge letter of November 22, 1972, he also begins with "One of my favorite ladies in this world is Beatrice L. Brown. . ." and he concludes with, "she goes forth with all my

BEE'S ILLNESS

good wishes for a future of a happy life with Marvin and her family."

During the next four years and the following almost six years, we lived practically a normal life. We entertained, socialized, vacationed abroad as well as in the U.S., and saw our family prosper and the grandchildren grow. Bee refrained from driving due to her right-sided loss of peripheral vision, but otherwise she accommodated herself to it. And she kept up with her local medical check-ups.

During the fall of 1977 Bee began complaining of severe pains in her upper back and numerous joints throughout her body. After X-rays ruled out arthritis, I had her consult Dr. John Jabbs, a rheumatologist in Syracuse. He performed many tests on Bee and gave her a complete blood work-up. He ruled out collagenous fibrous disease, and Bee was given the usual analgesics to relive her pains.

While in Syracuse on January 17, 1978, on our day off, Bee suddenly became weak with fever. Dr. Jabbs saw her at that time in his office and ordered her home to go to bed, believing she was coming down with the flu. She subsequently was treated by me and, with telephone consultations, by Dr. Daniel Adler in Syracuse for sixteen days. I had three blood cultures done during this time, all with negative results. Then she was hospitalized in Syracuse from February 5 to 14. Repeat examinations, including blood cultures, were all negative. The discharge diagnoses included, besides her cardiac condition, Recurrent Fever, etiology undertermined.

She was followed by both Dr. Jabbs and Dr. Adler, and after more tests she was diagnosed as having Polymyalgia Rheumatica. Then she was placed on the steroid medication Prednisone, which gave her some relief.

However, she continued with pains, and at times her mandibular joints were so affected that even chewing food became almost unbearable, so she subsisted on liquids and very soft foods.

HOUSE CALLS

Wanting another opinion late in 1978, I had her see Dr. Edward Sugarman, a Syracuse orthopedic surgeon. He suggested the non-steriod drug Tolectin and, although Bee was warned about its side effects, she wanted to try it, anything to make her more comfortable. And she did get considerable relief and continued with the medication until February 27, 1979. On that date, while we were sitting in our living room together after I had finished office hours late in the afternoon, she suddenly became extremely weak and pale. I aided her upstairs to bed and did an occult blood test on her stool, which was positive. With the help of Doris, I got her into my car, in the reclining passenger seat, and drove her to the emergency room of the Crouse-Irving Memorial Hospital in Syracuse. Dr. Hans Bruns, a gastro-enterologist, responded almost immediately, passed an endoscope into Bee's stomach and there found churning blood eminating from a diffuse lesion in the lining of her stomach. Evidently, the Tolectin had caught up with Bee and was causing a gastric hemorrhage.

Bee responded well to treatment with packed red blood cells and supportive medication. Despite Dr. Bruns's misgivings, he reluctantly discharged her on March 8th, because I had previously booked our flights to Palm Springs for two days later. The rest, warmth, and jacuzzi there in fact aided in her recovery from this event.

Bee did well for the next two years and again proceeded to live a comparatively normal life, and she lived fully every day.

In March of 1981 Bee began having problems with her vision. I came in to the kitchen for lunch one day, and she remarked that she was seeing double. She explained that she was looking across the street and the chimney on our neighbor's home looked like two of them, one on top of another. She was experiencing vertical double vision, which in medical terminology is diagnosed as amourosis fujax and often indicates a narrowing of an internal carotid artery in the neck. Also this could be caused by temporal

BEE'S ILLNESS

arteritis, a complication of polymyalgia rheumatica. I became alarmed and nervous, knowing complications of this syndrome could lead to a stroke.

Consultations between Dr. Jabbs, Dr. Leslie Woodcock, an opthalmologist, and Dr. Herbert Lourie, a neurosurgeon, were held, and as a result Bee had a biopsy done of her left temporal artery by Dr. Woodcock at the one-day surgical center of the Crouse-Irving Memorial Hospital on March 24. Fortunately this turned out to be normal. On her visit to Dr. Jabbs on March 31, her double vision was absent, and he reduced the daily dose of Prednisone, which he had recently increased, but had her continue with her other medication without change.

Bee continued to have visual difficulties and vertical double vision from time to time, so we set up an appointment with Dr. Lourie, who suggested a cerebral study be done. Remembering back to her coronary angiogram, which was a very unpleasant experience, Bee at first refused but then consented to have it done. She entered the hospital on April 20, had a cerebral angiogram and C.T. brain scan performed the next day, and was discharged on April 22. When I came to the hospital to take Bee home, Dr. Lourie took me to the X-ray department and explained the results of the tests. The series of X-ray films were placed in the view boxes, and he pointed out that a narrowing of approximately 50 percent in the left internal carotid artery was clearly demonstrated. He also explained that since the narrowing was within the skull, it was unapproachable and that surgery could not correct the defect. Bee had the right answer for this. "They do all kinds of tests on me, and all I get is that everything is normal or that nothing can be done." So with this behind her, it meant one more medical abnormality she would have to bear.

During this short hospital stay, Bee wrote the following note and presented it to me when I brought her home.

HOUSE CALLS

4/21/81, 2:30 A.M.

My Own True Love and My Beloved Family

One of these times I may not go home from the hospital or not awaken, and each time during one of these experiences I think I wish I'd said the words of how I feel.

No matter what or when, please know I think I've been the most fortunate of women. I've had a beautiful happy and productive life with loved ones and challenges making always to work for and to enjoy.

I only wish that you all well know that when I "go" I want you to be sorry, but not to mourn—remember me as I do my parents, with gratitude that I was fortunate enough to be their child—a couple who had the same deep love you and I have, Marv—what more does one really need—except a sense of humor?

I'm so happy to know I enjoyed and loved bringing up my sons, that we had so much fun and growth together.

No mother could be more pleased with the girls her sons chose—each one is *right* for the one she is married to.

It is good to love the daughters brought home to us and to have the delight of beautiful, bright, talented grandchildren who enrich the family love we have.

We always, you and I, Marv, have been happy to have had a daughter in Gerda, and she couldn't be more a daughter if I had given birth to her.

How wonderful and good this life has been—full of the meaning of living and loving and the knowledge that there is, in spite of all the strife and hatred in the world, a continuity of the Good and Blessed.

Jackie dear, you are and always will be my beloved baby sister.

Reading this over I've rambled and really haven't expressed all my thoughts but I'm glad I finally put on paper some of what I feel—my love of God and man—and above all my own dear dear ones.

A gratefully happy and content wife, mother, grandmother, and plain relative.

While Bee was being seen by Dr. Lourie she pointed out to him the worsening of movement of her right hand accompanied by numbness of the thumb and by wrist pain. He made a diagnosis of carpal tunnel syndrome and suggested surgery. Bee put it off for several weeks before she had it done.

While we were in the process of selling our home and property and my practice in Cleveland, we again decided for a change of pace in early 1982. So Bee left for Phoenix to be with the Terry Browns on March 4, and I joined her on March 25.

Bee enjoyed being in the warmth of the desert in Paradise Valley. She visited friends, lounged in the sun, and spent several days with our old friends from Central Square, Arthur and Madeline Wilson, who were living in Mesa. One day Bee and Janis flew to Los Angeles and back where she visited with her relatives and saw her Aunt Ella and Uncle Billie in nursing homes. Her greatest enjoyment, though, was being in the company of our grandchildren Jennifer and Lauren, both of whom were growing up and developing into beautiful youngsters.

When I arrived in Phoenix, I spent my time resting, reading, walking with Bee, visiting with two girlhood friends of Bee, and playing tennis. I remained there with Bee for five days, and on March 30 we left for St. Louis. Harriet picked us up at the airport, and we remained with the Miner Brown family until April 4, when we left for Cleveland. Bee felt like she was away for months, she seemed rested, relaxed, and ready to enter the final phase of our lives in Cleveland.

However, the remaining days on the North Shore proved to be very difficult for both of us. Bee was hospitalized three times, and I carried on my practice, finalized both the selling of my practice and the purchasing of our condominium in Syracuse, started to pack, ran a garage sale, and went through the legal procedures of closing a medical practice.

On Friday, April 16, Bee woke up with a choking feeling in her throat, difficulty in breathing, and considerable pounding in her chest. When I examined her, the one finding that disturbed me was that her heart was pounding at a rate of 140 beats per minute and that it was beating with many abnormal beats. I

HOUSE CALLS

contacted her personal physician in Syracuse, Dr. Daniel Adler, and he advised me to keep in touch with him but not to worry as long as the rate did not go over 140. So during the day, in between seeing patients, on numerous occasions I went upstairs to check on Bee. Her heart rate would drop to 110, 120 then back to 140. In the evening I began to get worried and concerned, because Bee was beginning to act uneasy. I called Dr. Adler again and told him, without asking, that I was bringing Bee into the emergency room of the Crouse-Irving Memorial Hospital. He met us there about 10 P.M., checked Bee, observed her for about an hour, and sent her home, reassuring me again that she would be all right and that her heart rhythm would revert to normal.

I didn't sleep very much that night, and I didn't sleep much the following two nights because there occurred no changes in Bee's heart rhythm and rate. After office hours on Monday night, Bee began to have some rales (abnormal sounds) in her chest, so I called Dr. Adler and again took Bee to the emergency room at the Crouse-Irving Memorial Hospital. Dr. Adler saw Bee and then asked if I wanted another cardiologist's opinion. I responded in the affirmative, and Dr. Anis Obeid came in directly. After a chest X-ray was taken, and several other tests were performed, he admitted Bee as a bed patient at 2 A.M. Tuesday.

She was monitored closely, given the appropriate medications, and gradually improved. I believe that with the necessary treatment a full-blown cardiac failure was averted. When I took Bee home from the hospital on April 29, she wondered out loud how long she could put up with all her close calls. And I replied, casually, "Bee, with your luck you will outlive us all." She looked at me inquisitively.

On May 5, I was awakened at about 2:15 A.M. by a steady light tapping noise. Bee was tapping on the wall in the bedroom using a slipper with her left hand. Her right arm and hand were useless. I immediately got out of bed and went into her room. Her bed sheets were half on the floor, and when I turned on the light I looked a her, frightened, and she looked up at me and said, "Marsh, I'sh had a shroke." Her speech was garbled, and her right arm and right leg were flaccid, without any response.

For the past three years she had been sleeping in the guest room and I in our bedroom. I generally left my bedroom door open, but the door separating our end of the upstairs from the other bedrooms was kept closed as was the guest room door. In this way Bee avoided the ringing of the telephone during the night, and her sleep was made as uninterrupted as possible. There was a bell near her on the night table, but she had knocked it over.

When I assessed the situation I called our North Shore Ambulance which arrived in about five minutes, called our Rabbi, called Doris Marcellus, then called the ever-ready emergency room and asked the clerk there to notify Dr. Obeid because Dr. Adler was away, and as soon as Bee was loaded into the ambulance I followed in my car. When I arrived at the emergency room Rabbi Ted Levy and his wife, Ina Rae, were already there, as was Doris. Dr. Obeid was on his way.

When I got to Bee's bedside in the holding area her speech was improved and understandable, and her right leg and arm were showing some reponse. When Dr. Obeid arrived, an emergency CT brain scan was done which showed a localized infarct in her left occipital lobe, and it ruled out any spreading hemorrhagic lesion. This finding made us all feel better. Both Rabbi and Ina Rae gave me and Bee great support. They encouraged Bee to keep up her improvement, and after things seemed stabilized they left for home about 4 A.M. Doris returned home then too, and I began again to breathe easier and left for home about 5 A.M., after Bee was admitted to Dr. Obeid's service and settled in her room.

I was able to get some rest, got myself breakfast, and at 9 A.M. was ready for another day of family practice.

I kept in contact with the hospital during the day, and each time I called I was told of her improvement. When I visited

197

HOUSE CALLS

her in the hospital in the early evening both her motor and sensory functions were returning to normal. By the end of the next day she had a practically full recovery.

Then she told me what had occurred. She was awakened about 1 A.M. due to a numbness in her right side. She tried to get out of bed on the right side but was unable to do so because of the paralysis of her right arm and leg. She tried to call out but her voice was too weak. Then she grabbed hold of the sheets and bed coverings with her left hand and inched herself slowly, pushing with her left leg at the same time. She finally got to the edge of the bed on the left side. She grabbed for the bell but when she pulled the lace doily on the bedstand the bell fell to the floor with it. She was afraid to go any farther for fear of falling to the floor. And she was exhausted, all this maneuvering having taken about one hour. She reached down to the floor and luckily came up with a slipper, and with this she started to pound on the wall, and I heard the noise. It was quite a traumatic experience for her.

Bee did very well. She improved daily, began ambulating in two days, her heart rhythm became regular at a rate of 70 to 80 beats per minute, and she was discharged on my seventieth birthday, May 15, 1982.

I was able to obtain the services of a nurse's aid out of Oneida to help Bee with her convalescence. She worked an eight hour day, made up Bee's bed, brought her her trays, and made her as comfortable as possible.

Bee's progress continued and although she was disappointed in not being able to partake in the packing procedure and our garage sale, after we moved to our new condominium in Syracuse on July 1, she took over the unpacking and settling of our new home. Here we were hoping to live our retirement years in peace and comfort, spending time with old friends as well as new ones, for me playing tennis regularly, for Bee playing bridge regularly, and doing some travelling.

With some minor restrictions, our lives again returned to

a new normalcy, always with the hope that it could continue.

Soon we were looking forward to Jennifer's Bat Mitzvah, which was scheduled for April 29, 1983. Arrangements for our stay in Phoenix for the months of March and April were made, and we started our driving across the country on February 25. Bee suggested we go by car in order to see more of the country.

The trip was uneventful, but when we arrived we were confronted by the news that Jackie, who with her husband was spending the winter in Phoenix, was seriously ill at the Scottsdale Memorial Hospital. Therefore, as soon as we were settled, I immediately went to the hospital, and after visiting Jackie and looking at her charts, returned to inform the family that her condition was critical. Her continual and distressing smoking habit had finally caught up with her, and she was in the intensive care unit with all types of supportive treatment being given her for advanced emphysema, or chronic obstructive lung disease. We visited her daily, but she deteriorated gradually and expired on March 19. This was a tragic loss to the family, but we managed to go on, and Jennifer did us proudly as she celebrated her day.

We spent the winter of early 1984 in Florida at the Palm Bay Club on Siesta Key, off the coast from Sarasota. One of the reasons for this change was that Bee didn't want to return to Phoenix since her loss of Jackie there, and also because she wanted to visit a cousin of hers, Emma Doak, who was living in Sarasota with her husband Russell. I played tennis there daily, took long walks on the hard surfaced sandy beach, we lounged on the beautiful white sand of the beach, Bee played bridge with newly found friends, we went out to dinner nightly, and we had an all around superb holiday. During all this time Bee was under good medical control, taking her medication regularly and getting her blood tests at a nearby laboratory in order for me to control her drug dosage. She was enjoying every minute and day of living.

Back home we both kept enjoying ourselves, and Bee seemed

HOUSE CALLS

to be getting along satisfactorily as long as she lived within her physical limits. During these months I acted in the capacity of Prison Physician for the Onondaga County Penitentiary and also conducted Well Child Clinics for the County Health Department. But soon we were making plans for the upcoming Bat Mitzvah of Terry's and Janis's second daughter, Lauren, which would occur on February 16, 1985.

We almost didn't make the trip because on January 14, 1985, Bee suffered another T.I.A., a transient ischemic attack. I arrived home from my jail work about 11:30 A.M., and as I walked in the bedroom where Bee was making up our bed she acted peculiarly, was placing the sheets in the wrong places, looked at me as though I was a stranger, seemed confused, and was disoriented. Therefore, I immediately took her to the hospital where Dr. Obeid took over again.

Bee again responded well and in twenty-four hours seemed to recover satisfactorily. Neurologic consultation was held, and the cause of this episode was blamed on either the narrowing of her left internal carotid artery or her polymyalgia rheumatica, or both. She was discharged in good neurological status on January 23. I hedged on going to Phoenix, but Bee insisted, so we went through with our plans.

We had reservations at the Olive Grove in Phoenix, where we had been two years earlier. This time we went by air, and we arrived there on Februay 5. Bee was feeling well and was looking forward to Lauren's day with great anticipation. Until the day of the event we rested, visited Terry and his family, visited with some Syracuse friends, and met the arrival of some relatives and of Miner and his family.

On the evening of February 15, Terry and Janis held a dinner party for the family in their garden around the pool. It was an unusually warm evening, and we all had a great time. That night we were driven to the Olive Grove, and we were to be picked up in the morning to proceed to the Temple for Lauren's Bat Mitzvah. We went to bed, hoping to get a good night's sleep.

About 4 A.M. I was awakened by unusual but familiar sounds from Bee's bed. She was having difficulty breathing and her respirations were noisy and fast. She was sitting up and said, "Marv, I guess I'm hyperventilating." I grabbed my stethoscope, listened to the loud, bubbly, wheezy rales in her chest, then contacted the desk, ordered an ambulance and dressed as quickly as possible. Bee, for the first time, was in acute congestive heart failure, her lungs were in pulmonary edema, and she was getting worse by the second.

Luckily the voluntary ambulance and paramedics on call were around the corner from the Olive Grove; their ambulance was housed in the Fire Department building. They were in our room in five minutes. I told them of the urgency of the situation and instructed them to get Bee to the nearest hospital as quickly as possible. And, fortunately, with the Humana Hospital only a few blocks away, and with the streets deserted, Bee was in the emergency room there in less than ten minutes.

By this time Bee was unconscious and close to death. Again luckily, a cardiologist, Dr. Thomas F. Ross, was in the intensive care unit on an emergency for one of his patients. He responded immediately to the physician on call in the emergency room and took over Bee's care. The two of them worked over Bee, resuscitated her, and then Dr. Ross intubated her by placing an endotracheal tube in her larynx below the vocal cords so that oxygen could be given to Bee directly into her lungs. Then Bee was transferred to the intensive care unit for follow-up care and treatment. Her life had been saved, but her condition remained critical.

While the doctors were working over Bee, I remained close by in the emergency room, thinking of the possibilities of Bee's recovery. After her transfer to the I.C.U., I was allowed to see her. Evidently the endotracheal tube was difficult to insert because bloody mucous was oozing from around it, down the corners of Bee's mouth, and down her cheeks. She was being monitored closely from both external and internal heart connections, had a continuous intravenous infusion into which medications could be inserted, and had a catheter in her bladder so that her urinary output could be measured.

She was semi-conscious at this point. I went into the adjoining waiting room, sat down, and prayed by myself for Bee. About 6 A.M. I called Terry who notified Miner, and soon both were at the hospital to visit their mother. At first Terry questioned the possibility of cancelling Lauren's Bat Mitzvah, but I insisted it go on as scheduled. So it did, while Bee was fighting for her life at the Humana Hospital.

The first four days were critical, and I notified Neal and Stephen in New York to come to Phoenix. They were put up at the Olive Grove. By the week's end Bee was stabilized and was recovering from her acute affair, so Neal and Stephen returned home, and Bee was transferred to a private room. She was discharged on March 1.

We resumed our stay at the Olive Grove. I took trays up to Bee for her meals, assisted her with bathing and dressing, had an oxygen tank for her, and transported her in a wheelchair. She gradually improved, and I was able to take her outdoors to expose her to the sunshine and warm air. As soon as she was deemed able to travel, I made the necessary arrangements to return to Syracuse, obtaining permission from the airline medical authorities to provide her with oxygen. We flew home on March 20, and Rabbi Levy met us at the Syracuse Airport. Bee was so happy to be in her own bed again and thanked God for giving her more time for living.

We were fortunate to obtain the services of a woman for cooking and helping with the household tasks, and later, after her niece graduated from high school in June, she came to help Bee, who by then was able to take over the cooking and perform some household duties.

Bee did well and was able to get out, visit her physicians' office, and go to the laboratories regularly. She did very little socializing, but friends stopped in occasionally to visit with her. She took oxygen regularly as well as her numerous supportive medications. I shampooed her hair and cut her toe-nails. I did all the grocery shopping, cleaned up in the kitchen, and I continued with my regular assignments at the County Penitentiary and at the Well Child Clinics—besides getting in some tennis.

So life went on, though somewhat precariously. I knew, and Bee sensed, what a resuscitation and an intubation could mean. We were on the edge of a waterfall, waiting and wondering when the raging water would take us over it to the rocks below.

We enjoyed the spring, summer, and early fall months. Bee's laughter and personality took over again, and we loved every minute of being together. And when she got dressed and put her make-up on, her friends would always comment, "How beautiful you look."

But it didn't continue. Again at 4 A.M. on November 11, 1985, Bee became restless, and even with increasing the oxygen supply, she became increasingly more dyspneic. I took her to the hospital in my car, having her sit up in order to help her breathe easier. Again she responded and was able to leave for home on November 27, 1985. Stephen and his family came to visit Bee during this hospitalization, and it seemed to ease the pain and give Bee more incentive for keeping her life going.

Approximately four months later, the same degree of heart failure occurred, and Bee was hospitalized from March 29 to April 4, 1986. And again, I was able to transport her in my car, this time at 6 A.M.

During the following four months, Bee spent most of her time at home. She took oxygen regularly, was able to go to her hairdresser once a month and have her nails done, and I took her out for rides about the country and out for dinner two or three times a week. At the same time I arranged for an outing in July for our Temple's senior group and was finalizing plans for my fiftieth medical class reunion which would take place the weekend of October 17, 18, and 19.

HOUSE CALLS

It was inevitable that Bee's will to live and her bodily resistance could not continue. And every time Bee came back, my telling her that "with your luck you'll outlive us all" could not hold out too much longer.

Thus again at 4 A.M. on August 5, 1986, I was awakened suddenly by respiratory wheezes made by Bee, who was having marked difficulty in breathing. This time she could hardly move herself to an upright position. I called an ambulance, which responded in a few minutes and transported her to the hospital again. There she was resuscitated and intubated again and treated for four days in the Coronary Care Unit and then in the Progressive Care Unit. She recovered sufficiently to be discharged on August 12.

Eleven days later, at 6 A.M. on August 23, Bee was back again in the hospital. Again by ambulance, and again she had to be resuscitated and intubated. This proved to be her final hospitalization. And this time she failed to respond as she had on previous visits. Soon the Labor Day weekend was upon us; Bee's critical condition summoned the boys with their wives, who were soon all around her bedside in the intensive care unit. On the third day of their arrival I was called at home early in the morning and told that Bee had pulled out her tubing, voluntarily or involuntarily, and that she was being resuscitated again. When I walked into the I.C.U., she had been revived again, and the intubation tube was again in place. The boys and their wives remained two more days, then I was left alone with Bee. So I resumed my daily telephone calls to them as well as to Gerda in Vienna.

During all these days we communicated with Bee by written notes. Gradually her writing became almost unintelligible, but we understood each other. After eleven days of being intubated, her tubing was removed, and her larynx, practically destroyed, made her voice come through in a muted whisper. And one of the first messages she got across was, "I want to go home."

So I contacted Doris Marcellus, who agreed to come to

BEE'S ILLNESS

our home from Constantia daily to help in the care of Bee. I was assured of a continuous supply of oxygen at home for Bee's support, and I had the necessary medication, including intravenous diuretics. Therefore Dr. Obeid discharged Bee on September 16, 1986.

During these eleven days of being intubated, Bee's only nourishment was provided by intravenous fluids and Ensure, a thick liquid, which was given her through a tube placed into her nose and ending in her stomach. She therefore lost considerable weight, her cheeks and face became thinner, and her extremities, especially her legs, became spindly.

It was a cool September day when I took her home from the hospital, so the nurses who dressed her also put the liner back in her raincoat. We got her into my car, and soon I entered the garage at our home. The door from our garage led into the eating area of the kitchen. Bee extended her legs out of the car, and as I tried to assist her she started to go down like a rag doll. Her legs could not support her. I picked her up in my arms and, with her arms about my neck, started for the door into the house. I over-estimated myself, and as we arrived at the transom my strength gave out, and we both went down to the floor. Bee remarked in a whisper, "Marv, after all these years you finally carried me across the doorway into our home." And we both laughed out loud. Then I removed her coat and then was able to carry her to her bed, help her undress and get into a nightgown, and get the oxygen started. Once more she remarked how lucky she was to be home and in her own bed. Doris arrived soon afterward, gave Bee a bed bath, made her as comfortable as possible, and then prepared lunch for us. She not only provided nursing care for Bee during the day, but also did the cooking for lunches and dinner at night.

I prepared breakfasts for Bee and myself, did the shopping, and took care of Bee after Doris left at 7 P.M. until 11 A.M. the next morning. I regulated the oxygen, prepared a schedule for Bee's medications, and gave her intravenous diuretics. Because

HOUSE CALLS

it was difficult for Bee to ambulate, I rented an aluminum walker for her, and with some support she was able to get around the bedroom, into the dining room and into the bathroom, avoiding at times the use of the bedpan. The days I conducted clinics I always left a phone number where I could be reached.

So we proceeded in this way for several weeks. Bee held up very well, but at times seemed to be on the edge. We had considerable pillow talks, and she repeatedly said how wonderful a life she had with me, that she was a completely satisfied and fulfilled woman, how our lives were enriched by having a daughter in Gerda, and with four wonderful sons, our beautiful daughters-in-law, and thirteen wonderful grandchildren. And she also said again that one day she would go to sleep and not wake up.

The weekend of my fiftieth medical reunion was soon upon us. Nine of my classmates out of a total of forty-six of us who graduated from the Syracuse College of Medicine in 1936 returned. The schedule called for a Friday morning of teaching, an early afternoon of lunch and visiting, then the Weiskotten lecture followed by the presentation of the Syracuse Medical Alumni Association's "Distinguished Alumnus" award. In the evening our class dinner was scheduled to be held at the Corinthian Club, a private women's club close to our home; on Saturday a clambake would be held; and on Sunday a brunch would complete the weekend.

Bee seemed excited about the weekend, because she always looked forward to visiting with my classmates and their wives. But I tried to keep it in low key because I couldn't see how, in her condition, she could attend any of the affairs. I decided to remain with her Friday afternoon, not meaning to attend the reunion functions until the dinner at night. About 3 P.M. she said, "Marv, you'd better go and be with your classmates now. You should get out of the house for a while." She insisted, so I dressed and left for Weiskotten Hall. When I arrived the lecture was just about finished, and so I entered the lecture room to sit with some of my classmates.

BEE'S ILLNESS

There were a few minutes of intermission, and then Dr. Jack Yoffa, the President of our Alumni Association, began his introduction of the "Distinguished Alumnus." He started out slowly, but as he proceeded, I gradually got the message. He was speaking of my career. As he said, "Well, today we will honor a home-grown talent. I am proud to be standing here to introduce a member of our golden anniversary class as our Distinguished Alumnus," he was speaking about me. Of course I felt honored—but completely flabbergasted. I was taken completely by surprise. After he finished his introduction, I was asked to come to the podium to accept the prize that went with the award, a gold-headed cane. And then, after making some remarks and accepting the congratulations from my colleagues, I drove home as quickly as possible. When I entered our bedroom I found Bee completely dressed in her blue lace dress, her make-up on, and, after telling her that she looked beautiful, I told her of the award. "Who else would they give it to?" was her reply. Then she remarked in no uncertain words, "I am going to the dinner tonight."

So she learned of my award, and somehow I got her to the dinner. With the help of a couple of my classmates we carried her in and she sat next to me in her beloved Corinthian Club. She was subdued, but her smiles came through, and she enjoyed every minute. On arriving home she collapsed on the bed and had to be undressed, and with help from Mrs. Wickman, the wife of one of my classmates, we got a nightgown on her. She then smiled, looked up at us, said what a great time she had had, and immediately fell into a deep sleep.

She awoke suddenly about 1 A.M. in moderate heart failure; and, after increasing the oxygen flow and injecting a diuretic into her vein, she went through the remainder of the night satisfactorily. That afternoon she insisted I go to the clambake, which I did for about an hour, and again I was introduced as the "Distinguished Alumnus" for 1986.

The following ten days and nights were difficult. I think

they were more so for me than for Bee. She was accepting the inevitable, and I couldn't. She seemed to do fairly well during almost all these days, spending them in bed, getting up to have her meals on television tables and, with help, walking to the bathroom. She watched television, napped, and had some visitors. And during the nights she would ask for more oxygen, and when I would tell her that she was getting the limit, she would answer, "Whatever is to happen will happen." Sometimes I would give her more diuretic.

And so at 4 A.M., her time, on October 28 I was again summoned for immediate action. She couldn't breathe well propped up in bed, so I eased her off of it into a straight chair and proceeded to inject her with more diuretic. But her left arm became limp; and, as I entered the vein with the needle, instead of the medication entering her vein, because of the limpness of her arm, the blood flowed out and onto the chair. I put her back in bed with her head on the pillow, she breathed two or three more times, I heard a gurgle in her throat, and then she breathed no more. I then listened for any heart beats, and hearing none with my stethoscope, said to myself, "She's gone." I looked at the clock; it was 4:20 A.M.

I kissed her on the cheek and removed the wedding band from her left ring finger, which I had placed on it almost fifty years ago. Then I called her attending physician, the undertaker, Rabbi Levy, and our sons and later in the morning our near relatives and close friends.

I received a letter of condolence from Eric Frey, one of our foster grandsons, and in it he expressed so much of the loss we all feel without my Bee. Among other statements he wrote, "It was so wonderful to talk to Grandma on the phone during the holidays. I was so glad to see her live into another year. Although God had sealed her passing away already at that time, there was still the sound of hope in her voice. Her last words to me were, 'I will dance at your wedding.' And I know that in my heart and in my thoughts she will dance wherever

I go and whatever I do."

And I'm sure these thoughts and sentiments apply equally to all our grandchildren. Bee will continue to dance, smile, and laugh wherever she may be.

Afterword

It would have been lovely to have fulfilled Miner's prediction and celebrated fifty years in practice in Cleveland, but in the event, I fell short of this goal by six years and two months, retiring on July 1, 1982.

I was still healthy and vigorous, and still enjoyed my work, but I was beginning to tire of being constantly on call. In 1976 I had hired Jeff Lape, a Registered Physician's Assistant, to help me in my practice, and he had proved to be competent, compassionate, and energetic. A move intended to win me a little free time, however, had an almost opposite effect; with professional help at last, my practice simply expanded to fill both of our schedules, leaving me, if anything, busier than before. Moreover, with my office forming a wing of my house, turning patients away proved impossible; when someone sought me out with a problem, I had to help. It seemed it had to be all or nothing.

I had a much more pressing reason for retiring than my own fatigue, however. I wanted to spend as much time as possible with Bee. Our large house had become too much for her to manage, even with help. Also, after years of putting the practice first, I decided it was Bee's turn.

In 1982, therefore, we sold the house and practice and moved

AFTERWORD

to Syracuse. Leaving Cleveland was a wrench for both of us, but the decision to do so paid off in the more than four years Bee and I were able to share with each other, our children, and our grandchildren. And the family (including Gerda and her two oldest sons) was able to celebrate at a wonderful seventieth birthday party for Bee on the Memorial Day weekend of 1974 at Neal's farm in the Catskill Mountain area of Livingston Manor. This has been added to the hundreds of memories I treasure of the good times Bee and I had during our almost fifty years together.

Bibliography

American Academy of Family Physicians Reporter 10, no. 12 (December 1983).
Badaway, Shawky Z. A., M.D., Jack Yoffa, M.D., Brent Fletcher, M.D., and Thomas Simon, M.D. "Uterine Tumor due to Placenta Increta." *New York State Journal of Medicine* (August 1985).
Beamish, Joe. "City Life." *Syracuse Herald Journal*, February 1, 1949.
Bullawa, J. G. M., M.D. "Serum Therapy of Pneumococci Pneumonia." *Journal of the American Medical Association* (December 18, 1937).
Cecil, Russell L. "Present Status of Serum Therapy in Pneumonia." *Bulletin of the New York Academy of Medicine* 15(1939): 104.
DeKruif, Paul. *The Sweeping Wind: A Memoir*. New York: Harcourt, Brace & World, 1962.
Encyclopedia of Jewish History: Events and Eras of the Jewish People. New York: Facts on File, 1986.
Moffitt, Ellis M., M.D. *American Medical News* (October 12, 1984).
"Professional Liability in the '80's." Report 1 of the American Medical Association Special Task Force on Professional

BIBLIOGRAPHY

Liability and Insurance (October 1984).

Teteris, N. J., A. A. Lina, and W. J. Holaday. "Placenta Percreta." *Obstetrics and Gynecology* 47(1976): 155-185.

Wangensteen, O. W. "Therapeutic Considerations in the Management of Acute Intestinal Obstruction: The Technic of Enterostomy and a Further Account of Decompression by the Employment of Nasal Catheter Suction Siphonage." *Archives of Surgery* 26(1933): 933

Wangensteen, O. W. and John R. Paine, M.D. "Treatment of Acute Obstruction by Suction with the Duodenal Tube." *Journal of the American Medical Association* (November 11, 1983): 1532.

www.ingramcontent.com/pod-product-compliance
Lightning Source LLC
Chambersburg PA
CBHW021848090426
42811CB00033B/2186/J

9780879754488